Is Your Present Image Costing You Money? Take This Test and See:

1. What is the best image for an insurance executive? A plant foreman? A TV announcer?

2. A wealthy prospect has asked you to lunch at an expensive restaurant. Who picks up the tab?

3. Is a sexy wife—or husband—good for your image?

4. How can you make people think your basement office is a corporate skyscraper?

5. Why are banks and insurance companies built like impregnable fortresses?

If you don't know the answers—or if you do, but know you can never know too much about success—read this book. You can look like a winner, act like a winner, and be a winner —with that all-important winning image that will take you where you want to go.

Robert L. Shook

Winning Images

ILLUSTRATED BY MICHAEL SENETT

PUBLISHED BY POCKET BOOKS NEW YORK

ACKNOWLEDGMENTS

My gratitude to Ann Bertagnolli, who did a fantastic job of helping to prepare the text. Also special thanks to Dorothy Snow, who is the world's best copyreader! And my deepest appreciation to R. J., who kept little Michael occupied so that I could spend evenings and weekends at home to write; Carrie, who kept R. J. out of my hair; and Bobbie, who entertained Michael, R. J., and Carrie. And Annabelle, who *really* runs our home. Without their cooperation, I couldn't have written the book.

 POCKET BOOKS, a Simon & Schuster division of GULF & WESTERN CORPORATION
1230 Avenue of the Americas, New York, N.Y. 10020

To Belle and Herb,
with love

Contents

8 CONTENTS

Introduction

Everyone, and practically *everything,* will sooner or later develop an image. Because what other people think is important to individuals, corporations, and smaller businesses, *Winning Images* is a book about *why* and *how* you can go about creating the image that is "right" for you.

There are two schools of thought regarding "image-building." If you choose to follow the first, you can go about your normal business and not be concerned about your image, for one will develop automatically. If you are aware of the value of a *winning image,* you will decide to follow the second school of thought, and work diligently at creating the image you want while pursuing your main objective. Instead of taking for granted that the most effective image will result by chance, you will make a conscientious effort to build the best image possible in order to achieve the most effective results from your main purpose.

If you believe in the philosophy of this second school of thought, *Winning Images* may be the book you have been waiting for. But first, let me tell you what *Winning Images* is not about. It is not a book on advertising or public relations. Since there are thousands of professionals in both fields, I have no intention of attempting to explain a subject in which I am not an expert. Rather, as a businessman, author, and professional observer of American attitudes and lifestyles, I am presenting my thoughts and philosophies regarding image-building and how creating a winning image can help you accomplish many of your goals more effectively and quickly.

You may feel that being so concerned with what others think is insincere, that putting a major emphasis on image-building suggests a certain degree of phoniness. But in my opinion there is nothing phony about a concern that man has had since the beginning of time: how others react toward him. In order for us to build a better civilization, we must all have this same concern. Everyone and everything, including career men and women, business men and women, small businesses, corporations, political parties, cities, nations, religious groups, and races all have an image. *Winning Images* will attempt to help you establish yours so that it will work for, instead of against, you, and aid you in taking giant strides rather than tiny steps toward where you want to go.

Throughout this book, the necessity of building your winning image on integrity will be emphasized. Any image which lacks honesty will be revealed sooner or later, and when it is, you will rue the day you ever wanted to build an image on deceit. *Winning Images* is concerned only with how to project an image based on truthfulness. *Winning Images* contains no lessons about misrepresentations—such images have foundations that not only will eventually crumble, but will also stunt your efforts to build a winning image.

Three completely unrelated subjects demonstrate how influential a winning image can be: filtered cigarettes, the game of pool, and God.

Several years ago, smoking a filtered cigarette was considered effeminate. When the manufacturers of Marlboro cigarettes began a vigorous advertising campaign to sell their filtered cigarettes, they changed the attitude of smokers throughout the world. In their television commercials and magazine ads Marlboro showed virile bronco-busting cowboys, with their Marlboro tattoos, smoking filtered cigarettes. Soon America and the rest of the world began to accept the new image of the filtered cigarette, and male smokers everywhere started lighting up filtered cigarettes. Why? *Because the image was changed.* Even though this is not a book about advertising, it is important to note how ad men *can* and *do* influence images.

One's image of the game of pool is, for the most part, based on who plays it and where. The man who "shoots pool" at the poolroom is often thought of as a "bum," whereas the man who plays it in the game room of his elegant mansion is regarded as a "gentleman." Both are engaged in the same recreation, yet one is looked down on and the other is admired. Again, the image makes the difference.

Even though what we know of God stems from different traditions, sources, and historical events, He is the greatest of all images. While most people will admit to never having seen, heard, or touched Him, few will deny that He, more than any other source, influences their lives. Though no attempt will be made here to debate God's existence, it is important to recognize that He nevertheless exists as an image.

As you can see, our reactions to the filtered cigarette, the game of pool, and God are determined by the images they present. It is hoped that *Winning Images* will help make you aware of what image you can project in order to influence what others think about you.

In pointing out how images constantly influence our daily lives, *Winning Images* concentrates primarily on careers; however, mention is also made of how images can be important to large corporations and small businesses. And though there are other kinds of images which deal with cities, states, religions, races, and entire nations whose impact can range from that of mildly affecting the individual to altering the whole course of civilization, this book will concentrate only on those images with which you, as an individual, should be concerned. There will be no discussion about overdone or obvious images, and their influence on the individual, such as the role of mother or father.

At first glance, some of the suggestions made for developing a winning image may seem somewhat expensive. But after you fully understand the concepts outlined, your realization of their potential value will almost certainly relegate to secondary consideration any cost involved in implementing them. Further, most of the concepts have been geared to the viewpoint of those of you who, like the majority of us, are on limited budgets.

Finally, *Winning Images* calls attention to the ways in which images affect you directly as well as indirectly, and an awareness of these sometimes subtle influences enables you to see things as they really are. In today's complex society you will have a great advantage if you can sit back and observe what's going on around you *before* you react. I sincerely believe that *Winning Images* will not only serve your career needs, but will offer you a new way of life as well. *With a winning image you'll be a winner!*

"And don't forget to pick up a copy of *Winning Images* on your way home from work, dear."

What's in a Name?

What's in a name? That which we call a rose
By any other name would smell as sweet.
> —William Shakespeare
> *Romeo and Juliet,* Act II, Scene 1

Without question, a name can and does make a big difference to one's image. Certainly we all form distinct impressions when we first hear a name. Perhaps we respond because of the sound of the word or because of mental associations we make, but very definitely an image flashes in the back of our minds simply from the name itself.

To illustrate this point, I conducted a small survey in which I separately asked twenty male friends of mine if they would take out Harriett Finkelstein, a secretary who was coming in from out of town. Eight-

een of the twenty told me they were not available for
the blind date. A month later I asked the same men if
they would like a blind date with Jill Conners, another
secretary from out of town. Influenced by the name
alone, sixteen expressed interest in Jill and wanted to
know more about her. Poor Harriett, who might have
been the real knockout, missed her chance for a blind
date simply because of the image her name suggested.

Two young men were seeking the same position,
selling computers for the Pewter Computer Company.
Both men, Harry Pflug and Mark Gable, were the
same age, and, according to their résumés, they had
identical qualifications, educational backgrounds, and
past experience. Yet when the Pewter Computer personnel vice president had to decide between them, he
was influenced by the mental image he had created for
each applicant. Harry, who was visualized as being
short and wearing thick glasses, got a letter of rejec-
tion. But Mark, visualized as a tall, handsome man
who would make a better impression on the clients of
Pewter Computer Company, was accepted and flown
in to the home office in Atlanta. Obviously, their names
had nothing to do with their actual appearances, but
they had a lot to do with the images they created.

The Most Expensive Name Change in History

Some of the largest companies in America have
recognized that their names can and do affect their
images. Because the image they present to the public
ultimately determines their acceptance, these companies are concerned with choosing names that will

influence the public in a positive manner. For this reason, many corporations have changed their names, even though the procedure itself is very expensive.

On June 31, 1972, the Board of Directors of the Standard Oil Company (New Jersey) adopted a resolution recommending to its shareholders that the company's name be changed to Exxon Corporation. In November of that year, the company accepted this new name, and "Exxon," undoubtedly the most expensive name change in history, was on its way to becoming one of the most commonly used words throughout the world.

Why did the company go to such trouble and expense to make such a change? Part of the reason stemmed from a Supreme Court ruling of 1911 whereby the Standard Oil organization was dissolved into thirty-four unrelated units. Some of these companies were held to have acquired exclusive rights to use Standard Oil's name in separate parts of the country. Although Standard Oil domestic affiliates tried for a number of years to establish the right to use "Esso" as a national trademark, their efforts were opposed in court on the basis of the antitrust laws because "Esso" meant "Standard Oil" to the public. As a result, the company had to market its product under the names Esso, Humble, and Enco. Realizing it would be at a disadvantage until it could advertise nationwide under one trade name, the company began its search for a word that would identify both its products and its services. The name Exxon was invented in the company's ninetieth year. It succeeded in establishing a new public image that eliminated much confusion in customers' minds and allowed them to rely on a certain quality of goods and services. It also

increased the company's ability to recruit employees and to communicate with the government, press, and general public.

Finding this new trademark involved exhaustive research, experimentation, and examination. Approximately ten thousand names were produced from the computer, and from this number a list of 234 was developed. This list was further cut to sixteen names, and finally to eight. Linguistic studies were made on these final eight words in more than one hundred languages in order to insure that none of them had an actual meaning or any adverse connotations. Nearly 7,000 people were interviewed, including about 4,000 in forty different cities throughout the United States, and over 15,000 telephone directories were examined. After three years the name Exxon was chosen, not only because it was a memorable word but also because of its distinctive design (the double "x"). Furthermore, Exxon was found easy to pronounce in most languages, and it had no vulgar or objectionable meaning.

In order to promote the new name, $100 million was spent. To begin with, all Esso, Enco, and Humble signs for 25,000 United States service stations had to be replaced with the red, white, and blue Exxon rectangle. Then at least fifty other signs, including the large ones first noticed on the freeway and the small ones on the gas pumps, had to be changed. At least 300 million sales slips and other service-station forms had to be reordered, credit cards had to be replaced, and thousands of other things had to be restenciled or repainted. These included the emblems on trucks, plaques for 22,000 oil wells, and the names on 18,000 buildings, storage tanks, tankers, and other equipment.

Then, too, new stock certificates had to be issued to shareholders. (Approximately 224 million outstanding shares were held by more than 780,000 company shareholders.)

Unquestionably, this was the most expensive name change in history, but Exxon's management realized the importance of the company's image and was willing to pay for it. In 1975 Exxon was the country's number-one leader in sales ($44,864,824,000), in assets ($32,839,398,000), and in net income ($2,503,013,000). Since American business is undoubtedly the most competitive segment of our civilization, we must conclude that our number-one company certainly knew what it was doing when it made a $100-million name change. In other words, it knew what image-building was all about.

Other Major Name Changes

Cities Service Company is known to have spent $20 million boiling its advertising logo down to "CITGO." Although much less in comparison with Exxon's, the money was invested for the same reason. For both companies, the image presented to the public was the primary concern.

Such name changes are nothing new for American big business. In 1961 the Olin Mathieson Chemical Corporation spent $2.5 million in a corporate advertising campaign to become known simply as "Olin." Because of product diversification, the company no longer wanted to be identified as a chemical company. For this reason, and because of the many confusing identities that resulted from acquisitions and from the merger of Olin Industries and Mathieson Chemical Corporation in the mid-fifties, the company changed its name. In 1969 the legal name of Olin Mathieson Chemical Corporation became Olin Corporation.

In 1973 the giant aerospace and consumer's company, North American Rockwell, made a name change to Rockwell International Corporation. Over the years the name "Rockwell" had become synonymous with high-technology manufacturing in a variety of product lines—among them, space vehicles, missiles, airplanes, electronic calculating equipment, textile machinery, printing presses and graphic equipment, power tools, business machines, household appliances, automotive components—in addition to the water, gas, and parking meters the company had originally manufactured prior to Chairman Willard Rockwell, Jr.'s mergers and acquisitions during the past few decades.

After many names had been suggested by corporation identification experts, Rockwell and his top management team decided that the only really fitting name was Rockwell, the name of the company's "architect." (As Al Rockwell says, with a grin, "The name Rockwell seemed to have a nice ring to it.") But since it was felt that the corporation's new identity ought to reflect its multinational character, "North American" had to be dropped. Hence the company became known as Rockwell International.

During 1974 thirty-one corporations on the New York Stock Exchange changed their names. Among these were Columbia Broadcasting System, Inc. (CBS Inc.), First National City Corporation (Citicorp), Flying Tiger Corporation (Tiger International, Inc.), and National Cash Register Company (NCR Corporation). In 1975, a recessionary year, nineteen corporation name changes were made on the New York Stock Exchange.

The Retail Credit Company, the huge Atlanta-based investigating company, changed its name in 1975 to Equifax because the company felt that its original name did not accurately reflect its activities. The words "retail credit" had a connotation that limited the perception of the company's activities to a much smaller area than the services it actually performed.

Conclusion

Giant international corporations change their names to better fit the images they are after, and we can learn a good lesson from them. Obviously the larger and more complex the company, the more involved the name-changing. (The owner of Joe's Auto Body Shop would have to invest only a minimal amount of money in order to change the name of his shop to The Great American Body Shop. The lesson is, the name of either your company or your product makes a major difference in what you are trying to accomplish. This is true not only for naming businesses, but for anything to which a name must be given. All of us are influenced by the title of a new book or movie. After writing, in collaboration with my father, my first book, *How to Be the Complete Professional Salesman*,* I spent many days trying to decide on a title. *Building Sales Confidence,* the one I finally chose, was then changed by my publisher to the present title.

* Robert Shook and Herbert M. Shook, *How to Be the Complete Professional Salesman* (New York: Frederick Fell Publishers, 1974).

"Good morning, International Express Corporation."

I did not argue with my publishers—after all, this was only my first book and they had enjoyed much success with hundreds of titles before they ever heard of Bob Shook!

The Starting-a-New-Business Image

Perhaps one of the most difficult images to create is the one you want when you first start out in business. While there are certainly many other considerations, I believe it is imperative to put image-building at the top of your list. It is much better to start out with no image and to begin building one slowly than to allow the wrong image to develop and then be unhappy with it. After all, it is easier to build a new building on vacant land than to have to tear down an old one first.

A good example of starting a new business is the experience shared by my father and me when we began our insurance agency in Pittsburgh, Pennsylvania, in 1961. At that time my father was forty-nine years old and I was twenty-three. Because we could not afford to pay office rent during our first years in business, we established an office in the basement of my father's home, which was in a typical middle-class neighborhood on the east side of the city. Both of us sold during the week, and on the weekends I acted as a secretary (my father could not type). Each of us took turns being the janitor. We interviewed new salesmen on Sunday afternoons—never during the week because we couldn't afford to miss selling time in the field.

In less than fifteen years our small father-son partnership became known as Shook Associates Corporation, one of two subsidiaries of a holding company we later formed named American Executive Corporation, which also fully owns American Executive Life Insurance Company. Our basement "agency" became a marketing company with its own insurance company and sales representatives in twenty-five states. While there are many more successful stories about businesses that grew much more rapidly than ours did during that period, I attribute much of our success to the emphasis we put on our company image in those days.

When we first began to establish our business, my father and I spent many hours discussing the importance of a good winning image in order to help us go where we wanted to go and get us there as fast as possible. We both realized that two things were essential from an image point of view. First, in order to make our maximum number of sales, we had to develop confidence in our prospects by convincing them that we were reliable people who would be permanently in the business, that we would be around in the future to provide service for them. In view of the fact that we were in the service business that was known to have the highest turnover of salesmen, this image of stability was especially important. Our second concern was to appear successful in order to recruit other salesmen. We believed in the theory that salesmen want to work only for somebody who's successful,

"Of course, I'll have to submit it to the home office for approval. . . ."

because if the boss isn't making money, neither can they.

Since we represented a national insurance company and our product was never sold in the office but in the prospect's residence, we did not go out of our way to tell people that the office was actually in the basement of my father's home. We were careful not to misrepresent and if people did ask where our offices were, we would tell them, and add that we were in the process of trying to decide where we should open new offices. Then we would name a few downtown office buildings we were considering for relocation. At the same time, we were always careful to use the terminology a salesman who really did work out of expensive offices would use. For instance, we made statements such as, "I'll submit your application to our Pittsburgh executive offices, which will in turn process your papers and forward them to our home office in Philadelphia." If a prospect asked us if his application had been approved, we would reply, "Let me call our Pittsburgh executive office and have one of the girls check the files." While I am sure he had an image in his mind of a busy office at the other end of the phone, my mother, interrupting her household work, or my sister, a senior in high school, usually answered. And, although I am somewhat embarrassed to admit it now, if nobody was home, I would fake a conversation with the dial tone. Deep down, I *knew* how important it was for my client to believe that I could offer him stability and dependability. Because I also knew that I was going to be very successful in my business and that I could ultimately give my client exactly what he wanted, my conscience never bothered me. I always believed I would be able to give him more than his money's worth.

We had to recruit our salesmen by interviewing

them in the living room of our home on Sunday afternoons, so referring to our executive offices, which were, in fact, beneath us, was not quite so easy. Often we simply avoided discussing our Pittsburgh offices, and the men merely assumed that they were located somewhere downtown. We always carefully explained to each person we interviewed that, since our time in the field during the week was so important, we liked to interview in our home on Sundays. This explanation not only created an image that suggested we made quite a bit of money when we were out selling, but it also showed we were good family men who wanted to stay home on weekends. Naturally, the new salesmen eventually found out where our offices actually were, but by this time we had been able to prove to them that they could make money. By showing them new sales, we not only sold ourselves, but we gained their confidence as well. Whenever a man we were interviewing asked us point blank where our local offices were, we always told him the truth and emphasized that "the secret to making money in business is to have a low overhead." To this we frequently added, "In this business, since the customers don't come to you but you must go to them, who needs a fancy office? We certainly don't need to feed our egos by sitting behind a big desk just to impress guys like you who are looking for a job!"

Over the years I have witnessed many other small businesses that started in basements or even garages and later expanded to become very successful ventures. I vividly recall when Richard Tracy told me that he had finally made the big transition from his home to a small space in an out-of-the-way strip shopping center. Dick was a top office equipment repairman, so I asked him, "Did the new location make a big difference in your business?"

He replied, "All the difference in the world. Since I moved out of my home, I get three times the orders I got just five months ago." I said I was surprised to hear that, for I didn't think the new location would provide enough walk-in trade to make that much of a difference. Dick then told me he had very few walk-ins; however, moving from his home had so increased his present customers' confidence in him that they all started giving him larger orders. "It's amazing," he said, "that the same customers who never referred customers to me began to have their business associates and other department heads contact me for orders. It's as though I wasn't good enough to repair all their machines in the past, but now, suddenly, I have arrived!"

Another friend of mine, Dr. Dumoor, once asked me to rent him office space in a building I was proposing for construction in one of the most prestigious areas of Columbus, Ohio. Just finishing his residency at Ohio State University Hospital, he was about to embark on his new career as a plastic surgeon. When he gave me the details for the type of office space he wanted, I was amazed that the young physician was willing to spend so much money before opening the door to his first patient. But Dr. Dumoor explained to me: "In the field of plastic surgery you must create for your patients an atmosphere that suggests that you are not only successful, but that you have been practicing your specialty for many years. Nobody," he went on, "wants to have his daughter's nose restructured by an inexperienced doctor. For something less serious, like a malfunctioning liver or the removal of the left kidney, parents are not really that concerned about the doctor's experience. But when it comes to cosmetic surgery, they want to deal with a doctor who gets results."

When Dr. Dumoor finally did move into his new offices, he furnished them in a very traditional manner, suggestive of his practice having been established a long time. He had known another out-of-town plastic surgeon who had decorated his new office with very expensive "mod" furniture, and his practice never really got off the ground. The conclusion we drew was that parents did not want their daughters to be given a mod nose! I might add that Dr. Dumoor has a flourishing practice, and I have often wondered if his medical school offered a course called Image-Building 101.

Another good lesson in image-building can be found in my own personal experience with a young architect who had moved to Columbus from Los Angeles. Kent Clark was introduced to me by a good friend at a cocktail party, and I learned that he had graduated from one of the nation's finest universities. Since I was in the process of planning my new office building, I was quite anxious to find a new architect with fresh ideas. I also liked, whenever possible, to give business to promising young men and women who were embarking on new careers.

Kent set up an appointment to meet with me at my offices, and although he changed this date twice, he finally did arrive. I had been excited about seeing his portfolio, but was extremely disappointed when he showed it to me because it was so haphazardly put together. Though I had thought he was "setting me up" by canceling the first two interviews, he had delayed in order to make sure that his portfolio was in perfect order before I saw it. As much as I wanted to do business with him, he showed me nothing to convince me that he would be my man. In short, I had no idea whether or not he possessed any real talent. I finally had to express my concern about what he was actually capable of doing. "I need something concrete," I said, "to be able to make my decision about what kind of building you can put up for me. We both know there are many fine architects in this city who have constructed some outstanding buildings. All I have to do in order to see what they have done is get in my car and drive to their work. With you, I don't know. I must depend on what you show me from your portfolio. I have to be shown in black and white."

Kent became very indignant. "Mr. Shook," he said, "I just don't operate like that. I believe that my clients should be able to chat with me, as you have done, and, based on my ideas and my personality, they should be able to sense what I can create. I don't believe in commercializing my work by putting together a portfolio like you have suggested."

I tried to convince him that if I were a young architect (or, for that matter, a struggling artist or builder), I would spend weeks or months if necessary to develop the most sensational portfolio possible. After all, what else did I have to sell? My looks alone were not a good enough reason for somebody to want to spend $1 million or more on a new building! My attempts to help him were in vain, for he would not accept the advice I gave him.

Conclusion

Regardless of what field you are in, when you begin a new business, you must be concerned with your image in order to get where you want to get successfully and quickly. You must remember that you are competing with many established businesses that have proven track records, while you are an unknown quantity. In order to be able to compete effectively, you need an image, and you must carefully plan out the one you want. Don't wait for one to "happen" automatically. You'll eventually have an image whether you want one or not, but by conscientiously developing the right one, I strongly believe you will get what you want much more effectively and in a shorter period of time.

While it is important to know that a winning image is necessary for a new business, you must determine how much you can spend on this priority in relation to your available cost resources. For example, a struggling young attorney may want spacious, plushly decorated offices in the most prestigious new downtown high-rise, as well as a beautiful receptionist and secretary; but he probably cannot afford all these image-builders before he builds his practice. For this reason I recommend that the new entrepreneur not overspend in his quest to build the right image—but that he establish priorities and work within a reasonable budget. Always keep in mind the old adage: "In order to make money, you must spend money." Remember, in the beginning years of our business, my father and I were able to achieve a winning image by operating with a very low budget. Quite frankly, we started our business on the proverbial shoestring simply because we didn't have any other choice—we were practically broke!

3 Appearances and First Impressions

"You get only one chance to make a first impression."

Although I do not know who said it, I agree one hundred percent with the above quotation. Surely you must have suspected that a book entitled *Winning Images* would have a chapter on appearances. And you were absolutely correct, because appearances definitely have a great deal to do with your image.

I do not intend to recommend any such drastic changes as a face lift, a nose job, a hair transplant, or silicone injections in your breasts; but I do want to encourage you to be aware of how easily you can rectify some of the most obvious appearance images. In short, if you have a homely face, I simply want you to learn to make the best of your homeliness.

Dressing properly is the most obvious appearance image. Depending on what you do and in what part of

"Sure I realize how important your image is by the way you dress, but . . ."

the country you live, there is a right way and a wrong way to dress. Because there are so many different dress codes, the discussion here will be limited to those styles most appropriate for the executive-type male. However, the suggestions made can, with a little thought, be easily adapted to your own situation.

My philosophy has always been to dress in a relatively conservative manner when conducting business so that I would offend the least number of people. Since it is most important to have everything going for you in business, you cannot afford to wear clothes that might have an adverse effect on certain customers.

Sam Slade, a life insurance agent, is a good example of a person who precipitated this kind of negative response from the people he dealt with. He habitually wore leisure clothes, in which he felt most comfortable, and told me, "I dress to please two people—my wife and Sam Slade. You're out of date, Bob. In this modern carefree society, people do their own thing. I never liked to wear a suit and tie even as a little kid when my parents made me dress up to go to Sunday school, and now that I'm adult and don't have to, I won't!"

"Let me ask you a very important question, Sam," I said. "For an extra hundred dollars, or perhaps as much as two or three hundred per week, would you be willing to dress conservatively, as I do? Stop and think before you answer this. I'm talking about wearing Brooks Brothers–type suits, button-down shirts, a rep tie, and cordovan wingtip shoes every day you go to work."

"For that kind of money, I'd have to be a damn fool not to!"

"Well," I said, smiling, "it's impossible for me to know exactly how many important clients you turn off throughout the year because of the way you dress, but I suspect you're losing a great deal of money, perhaps thousands or tens of thousands of dollars each year in unmade sales. Those leisure suits you wear are definitely a luxury item because they're costing you a small fortune in terms of lost business!"

Sam looked worried. "Do you really think I turn off that many people with my mod clothes?" he asked.

"Absolutely," I replied. "This is particularly true of the business you've been trying to break into. The big sales that involve group, key men, partnership, retirement, and pensions generally mean dealing with an executive on the upper echelon. I'm sure you've noticed that most of these men who make important decisions dress the way I do. Since you rarely find them wearing leisure suits to work, you can conclude *they don't approve of that kind of dress for business*. On the basis of this conclusion, you can probably assume that their first impression of you will be a bad one because they will more than likely resent the way you dress. Since all businessmen place a high value on their time, they probably won't even let you give them a sales presentation. They must say no to most salesmen who call on them, and because they are selective, you'll be one of the first to get the axe before you even get your foot in the door."

"Okay," Sam said, "I'll go along with you when you say I turn off businessmen with my mod clothes. But what about when I call on a working man at his home in the evening, or on prospects who dress much the same way I do—like entertainers, hair stylists, and florists?"

"You can't afford to have your clothes decrease your odds in any way. Don't you think you're limiting your market potential by calling on just those types of prospects? It's my opinion," I added, "that you lose something even with the mod-type prospects because they, too, want to have complete confidence in the agent they're dealing with. They want to know you'll be around for a long time to give them service, and conservative dress signals this kind of stability. On the other hand, to many people the mod look suggests that you might be both flighty and mutable."

That my conversation with Sam had made a favorable impression on him was evident a few weeks later when I encountered him lunching with a business client. He was wearing a new pinstripe suit. On weekends and at cocktail parties, Sam continued to wear his leisure suits, but he was on his own time then, so I certainly couldn't criticize him, even though such clothes are not to my liking.

In his book, *Dress for Success,** John T. Molloy discusses an experiment in which he planted an actor in a New York City corporate headquarters and directed him to ask a hundred secretaries to retrieve files for him. With the first fifty, the actor wore black scuffed shoes with big silver buckles, a flashy blue-green suit, and a chintzy tie. Only twelve out of fifty secretaries would accept his order! For the second part of the experiment, the same actor wore an expensive blue suit, a white shirt, a silk polka-dot tie, and cordovan wingtip shoes. He also styled his hair. Out of the second group of fifty, forty-two secretaries retrieved the files he requested.

Molloy entitled his second experiment "The Beige Raincoat Experiment." As he states in his book: "Intuitively, I felt that beige raincoats were worn by the upper middle class and black by the lower."** Upon checking with the finer men's stores that catered to executives, he discovered they sold four times as many beige raincoats as black ones. When he inquired at the

---

* John T. Molloy, *Dress for Success* (New York: David McKay Company, Inc., 1975).
** Ibid., p. 15.

men's stores in working-class shopping areas, he found the ratio to be just the opposite. For his experiment, Molloy visited the offices of fifty executives and carried with him a copy of the *Wall Street Journal* in a manila envelope. He told the secretaries he had to deliver his package personally. When he wore the beige raincoat, he was able to deliver twenty-five packages in only half a day, but when he wore the black coat, he needed a day and a half to deliver the same number of packages.

As you might easily ascertain, Molloy shares my appearance philosophy.

Because I believe in it so strongly, I have often told my new salesmen that one of the best investments they can make is to buy themselves two expensive suits —one a pinstripe and the other a lighter gray, preferably with a vest. These two suits are worth more than a closetful of second-rate suits that lack style. If I were on a very tight budget, I would rather own these two suits and alternate them throughout the work week than purchase several suits that would not give me the image I wished to project. The secret is not quantity, but quality.

A similar line of thinking can be applied to hair. Certainly, hair styles change from year to year, and what was considered long hair in the fifties and early sixties is, by today's standards, quite conservative. The important thing to consider is neatness rather than length. The same holds true for beards and moustaches. Neatly trimmed, they can give you a very clean-cut look. However, handlebar moustaches and Fu Manchus hardly seem appropriate for an executive. If you insist on wearing either, you are hurting your image, and doing so is going to cost you money.

Another suggestion I've made to many salesmen and business executives who work evenings is that they carry a portable electric shaver in their briefcases. Before an important late-afternoon or early-evening business meeting that end-of-the-day, worn-out look, so detrimental to a positive first impression, can be eliminated by taking a five-minute break to shave.

In my book *Total Commitment** Dr. Denton Cooley is quoted as saying that trim physical condition and neat grooming are very important for a heart surgeon. "You can call it vanity, but I think it's really a matter of pride," he says. "I think it would destroy the faith my patients have in me if I were to give them medical advice about how to take care of themselves, and at the same time I was talking to them, I'd be fat and dumpy, with a cigarette hanging out of the side of my mouth. . . . Nobody wants to be operated on by a slovenly surgeon."

Equally important to a good appearance is your own *self*-image. Although I'm not being original when I say it, I'm sure you'll agree that the way you see yourself will reflect the image you portray to others. In a chapter on mental attitude in my first book** I suggested a hypothetical situation that can be appropriately applied in *Winning Images:*

Let's say that John, a top executive with a salary in the $40,000 to $50,000 range, has been painting his house all day and is covered with paint from head to foot. (Of course he doesn't *have* to paint his own house; but he *likes* to.) Dressed in old work clothes, he gives the outward appearance of a bum. At this point, he discovers that he's running low on paint, so he hops into his

* Robert L. Shook and Ron Bingaman, *Total Commitment* (New York: Frederick Fell Publishers, Inc., 1975), p. 236.
** Shook and Shook, *How to Be the Complete Professional Salesman,* p. 38.

car and goes to a nearby hardware store to pick
up an extra can. When he arrives, looking shabby
and dirty, a clerk walks briskly up to him and ad-
dresses him in the following manner: "Sir, may I
be of assistance to you?"

Now take another case. In this instance, a guy
named Bill—who just happens to be John's identical twin—walks into the same hardware store,
dressed in a similar manner, and is spoken to in
this way: "Hey, buddy, what can I do for you?"

Why was it that John was called "Sir" and was
treated as though he were an important person, while Bill was addressed "Hey, buddy"—as
though he weren't worth the clerk's time? Since
both men had identical physical appearances,
there must have been something else that made
John appear important and Bill insignificant.
That "something else" was John's *self-image,
which makes him feel important and which shows
through to the people he comes in contact with.*
His self-confidence has given him a certain posture, a certain way of walking and a certain look
in his eyes.

Bill's self-image, on the other hand, has made
him come across as an unimportant nobody. Obviously, that's the way he feels about himself. And
it *shows!*

Along with your own personal appearance and attitude about yourself, your business approach can
create a good first impression on your client. When
calling on a customer, it's very important that you
begin your conversation with him by getting right
down to business. He's not really interested in what
you have to say about the weather, last night's presi-
dential speech, or Sunday's football game. Neither is

he interested in being flattered about his beautiful offices, nice-looking suit, or the "knockout" he has for a daughter, whose picture is on his wall. (For all you know, the woman in the picture could be his wife or girl friend!) Such small talk is a form of insincerity and an intrusion on his time. I have always found it effective to get to the point, and I assure you that any businessman will respect you for doing likewise.

Just as appearances determine first impressions of individuals, so do they of products, places, and businesses.

For example, you've probably noticed that parking lot attendants of successful restaurants always park the Rolls-Royces, Mercedes, Cadillacs, and Continentals in the most conspicuous places so that you can't help but see them as you walk toward the entrances. I used to think this was done because wealthy people gave bigger tips, but the real reason is that every good restaurant man knows that *good images sell food*. He wants to tell the public: "We cater to discriminating people. It's obvious, therefore, that our food has to be excellently prepared."

Every retail store should always strive to have a clean look, for nobody wants to patronize a dirty-looking establishment, no matter how much quality is actually offered. And once a place of business gets a reputation of uncleanliness, it's very difficult to live down. Even for a businessman operating on a low budget, a freshly painted store doesn't involve much cost. Light colors can give a lot of extra mileage. Whether you own a corner grocery store, a fast-food hamburger operation, or a ladies' dress shop, bright colors will always lend a clean and cheerful appearance. Bright lights, both inside and outside the store, will have the same effect. If you can't afford a good janitorial service, then roll up your sleeves and spend

"I think this plastic umbrella is killing my image."

a few extra hours each week making sure that dust doesn't accumulate on your shelves or merchandise.

A neat and tidy appearance also suggests that you are efficient and well-organized—and there isn't a business I know of that doesn't want that type of image. If you've ever walked into a neat and orderly garage at a service station, I am sure that, as I do, you feel more comfortable leaving your car there to be serviced.

Conclusion

Throughout *Winning Images*, you will find many references to appearances and first impressions. In this chapter I have highlighted just a handful of instances in which appearance determined a first impression and greatly affected the desired image. You should be able to apply the philosophy across the board so that you can benefit from this message in other areas.

I sincerely apologize to the female reader for discussing only the appearance of men, but quite frankly, I do not have the expertise to advise women on how to dress. The same basic message, however, is equally applicable to you. I might add that you should avoid trying to look sexy on your job—unless, of course, you happen to be a hostess in an all-night massage parlor!

4 Your Image and Your Employees

Assuming that the average executive works a minimum of eight hours a day (when I semiretire I'll slow down to a forty-hour week), the actual time he spends with business associates is equal to or greater than the time he spends with his immediate family, and far surpasses the time he spends with relatives and friends. A typical businessman may socialize with his "best friend(s)" two or three evenings a month, but, at best, these get-togethers average only four hours each time. With relatives, this time may be only a couple of hours every other Sunday afternoon, if that much.

There is also the time spent participating in sports. But again, these take up limited amounts of time, and not a great deal of communication with others is involved.

Considering, then, the time spent "in the shop" and the value you place on your career, the people you work with are very important. Because business associates rank very high on my list of important people, as I am sure they do with other employers, this chapter is devoted to the role of the *boss*—which, incidentally, is a dirty four-letter word I never use.

In his relationship with his employees, the employer should be aware of and strive for many images. For the "leader," the most important image is that of the pacesetter. Whether you are the chairman of the board, president, senior vice president, department head, or foreman, one of your chief functions in your management capacity is to set the pace for subordinates. The best chief executive officers I have known are generally the first to get to work each morning and the last to leave. These top men have become achievers, not only because of their own hard work, but also because of their ability to motivate others to work hard. I would find it very awkward to ask a man to work several evenings a week if I left the office at five o'clock.

As the employer, you are not only the pacesetter, but you should also be the style-setter. This doesn't mean you should look like a fashion plate; but if yours is a business that must create a specific image for customers and clients, it is up to you to determine how this can be accomplished through the appearance of your employees. If your goal is to create an image of dependability and stability, for example, your employees must dress conservatively. But don't expect your young executives to wear button-down shirts and three-button suits if you come to work in sport shirts and jeans or leisure suits.

Without question, the best way to achieve your purpose is by example. Always be the do-as-I-do, not the do-as-I-say, type. William Graham, a highly successful developer of apartment and warehouse complexes and shopping centers, has made millions of dollars during the last decade. Although Bill appreciates and has the finer things in life, he has never purchased an expensive car for his personal use, though his wife and children drive Cadillacs and expensive foreign sports cars. Since he travels over a five-state area to visit the different projects he has under construction, I once asked him why he didn't have a big luxury car for comfort. "After all, Bill," I commented, "you certainly could afford to have the finest custom-made automobile, and it would be a hundred percent write-off in your business."

To this Bill replied, "Bob, if I were to drive around in a big air-conditioned Cadillac all day visiting my men who are working in temperatures sometimes exceeding a hundred degrees, they would have a very poor image of me. If they were half-exhausted and covered with perspiration, and saw me get out of an air-conditioned car in a clean, neatly-pressed suit, I believe they would lose their incentive to work." He smiled. "If you were the foreman, how would you like to see some big shot pull up in his fancy car and tell you, through a small opening of his window, that you were behind schedule and should make the men work faster at laying bricks? If I were that man, I'd want to throw a brick right through the car's windshield."

Setting the pace should be your objective in any kind of work, whether it's at a grimy construction site or in the confines of a clean surgery room. As Dr. Denton Cooley, the famous Houston heart surgeon, told me when I interviewed him for *Total Commitment,** "I try to set the pace that everybody will follow." Cooley insisted open-heart surgery, which requires twelve people, including nurses and the two persons necessary to operate the heart pump that

* *Op. cit.*, p. 234.

circulates the patient's blood when the heart is being worked on, is a team effort. He explained, "I want them to think that I did a beautiful job, and that they should carry on with the same excellence. If I'm going to be the captain of the team, I've got to provide leadership, operative procedures, and, of course, respect for my teammates' roles." Every leader, no matter what his profession, creates an image for his associates that gives them essentially the same message.

To create the right image for your employees, it is very important that you have *integrity*. In order to win their respect, you must demonstrate that your company is honest with both its customers and its associates. Nothing shakes the confidence of an employee more than seeing that his firm does not treat its customers fairly. Sooner or later his reasoning will tell him that "if my company can screw the customer, it can do the same to me." If I worked for Harry's Finer Meat Shop and was instructed to shave an ounce or two from every pound of corned beef sold, it would not take me long to suspect that what Harry had me doing to the customers he would someday do to me!

Several years ago at a cocktail party, I had a conversation with one Herb Humphrey, who said, "You know, I've never met an employee who could be trusted. If given a chance, they'll never fail to steal from their employer." Later in the evening, after a few drinks, Humphrey spoke to me again. "The insurance companies in America make crooks out of all businessmen," he said. "When a water line broke on our warehouse last winter, I made my boys hose down the merchandise because I knew the insurance company wouldn't pay the claim since there wasn't enough damage." He also added that as he enthusiastically instructed his employees to hose down the already damaged goods, he threw in a "few" undamaged but out-of-date items to include in his claim. This was the same gentleman who had been complaining to me that his employees were stealing him blind! Realizing that it would be a waste of time to tell him that he was getting exactly what he deserved, I simply walked away from him.

I can't overemphasize the importance of an employee's belief in the integrity of his employer, because without this, a business leader will eventually lose his ability to lead. You must always have people's faith and loyalty in order to be an effective leader. Once you lose this trust, you will not be able to delegate authority to, or generate enthusiasm in, your co-workers. Even in large corporations, where a great amount of teamwork is required, I believe it is impossible to rise to the top if you are not a team player. If you are to be effective as a team leader, people must *want* to help you get ahead, and if you lack integrity, you will never get the enthusiastic support from your staff that you need in order to rise in management. While it must be admitted that a man strong enough in other areas can sometimes "fool the people" and perhaps even make it to the top, this kind of man rarely stays there very long if he continues to lack integrity.

Less serious, but still important, is the businessman's common practice of "legally" paying many of his personal bills through his business. He makes a foolish mistake when he lets his employee see that the business pays when he takes his family and friends out to dinner or to the country club, or when he sends his daughter an airline ticket so that she can come home from college. Because the employer is getting away with something the employees can't, this kind of activity certainly has an effect on the employees' morale. I also believe you are setting a bad example if you ask your secretary to type your son's six-page English theme. She would be perfectly justified in thinking, "Why should I have to type Tommy's theme? That's not my job."

You should also be careful about asking your secretary to run your personal errands, though for the high-powered executive in the upper echelons of management, leeway in this respect can be granted. His time is worth hundreds of dollars an hour, and if he simply does not have time to do personal errands himself, he can ask his secretary to take care of them. Without question, "time is money" to every business in America, and since the biggest expense of any major company is not its inventory, its leases, or its other fixed overhead, but the salaries paid to employees, it is very important for each member of the team to place a high value on his or her time and waste as little of it as possible. Again, you, as the leader, must set the example. If you come into work late every day, don't expect your employees to come in early; and if you spend a great deal of time taking coffee breaks, you'll soon discover that the rate of coffee consumption in your office has increased for all your associates. Wouldn't you feel embarrassed to take an hour-and-a-half lunch break every day if you were a junior executive working under a man who never spent more than a few minutes eating the lunch he brought from home?

Another important quality to have when dealing with people is fairness. Your subordinates should know that you will treat them equally and not show favoritism. Nothing can destroy the morale of an office quicker than the promotion of an undeserving son-in-law or a dizzy redhead.

Whenever you do give a subordinate responsibility, also grant him the authority to go along with it. And you must always remember that your employees, as well as yourself, will eventually make mistakes. Even though such errors in judgment often cost your company a great deal of money, you must accept the situation when it occurs and explain, "Look, I won't deny that your mistake was a costly one, Jim, but we can't allow ourselves to get upset and quit because of it." I guarantee that you'll accomplish much more with this attitude than if you severely browbeat the man until he fears you and loses the courage to use his judgment in the future.

Bob Hall is a good example of a man who liked to run a "tight shop" and rule with an "iron hand." For thirty years he manufactured men's sport jackets, and he became a millionaire in the process. An adherent of the old school of thought that does not encourage trusting employees, Bob had occasionally attracted capable people, but he would not delegate them authority. He was "boss," and he was responsible for making all the decisions. Nobody was allowed to touch the morning's mail until Old Man Hall went through it himself. Although this procedure may not be so unusual in a small business, it certainly is in a business doing $7 million a year in gross sales.

Everyone in the company feared the old man. Even though it is customary for clothing manufacturers to give markdowns on merchandise at the end of a season, Hall would never tolerate important customers' requests for such discounts. Whenever his salesmen were forced to call from the office of an important buyer, Hall would never accept the telephone charges. If the call was paid for by the intimidated salesman, Hall would yell over the phone, "You tell that rotten SOB that I only give markdowns when I feel like it, and he has a lot of nerve to even ask. Tell the bastard to go to hell. If he doesn't want to do business my way,

then we don't need his business!" In spite of Hall's
wretched attitude his company did make money because he made a high-quality product. But a different
personality would have run the company with even
greater success, which is precisely what happened
when Hall retired. The outsider who bought him out
increased the business from $7 million to $16 million
in less than two years.

Many employers and executives are often concerned
about how close they should be to their co-workers.
This is a difficult subject to discuss because it depends
so much upon the individual personalities involved.
Nonetheless, there are two extreme types. The first is
the one who is buddy-buddy with everyone—he is not
effective in giving orders and delegating authority. His
problem is that he talks too much about his own personal concerns and intrudes into the personal lives of
others. The second is the executive who sits in his ivory
tower and completely isolates himself from the members of his staff. This deep-freeze relationship makes
his subordinates feel inferior, and they will eventually
despise him for it. As an executive, you must use your
discretion in determining a happy medium between
these two extremes.

It is very important that employees not only have a
winning image of their employer, but of their company
as well. Every employee must have faith in the long-
range growth of the company. If the company is going
backward, he can't help but realize that there won't
be many opportunities for him in the future. He
knows that aggressive and successful companies develop more people and offer them more opportunities
in management.

At the same time, your employees must believe that
the men at the top of the company are well compen-
sated, for then they have something to look forward

"Gentlemen, our chairman of the board will now address us on the subject, 'The Future Growth of Great American.'"

to themselves. If middle and top managers are not earning good salaries, those on the lower echelons will not expect to be well rewarded for their efforts. As long as you don't create a "playboy image," your subordinates will take pride in seeing that you have acquired the finer things in life, for this gives them the hope they, too, will someday possess such luxuries.

Since many field salesmen are very car-conscious because of the amount of time they spend behind the wheel, I think it is especially important that the sales manager drive a late model, high-quality car. As a status symbol to salesmen, the car is definitely a winning-image builder for the sales manager, even though it may not be personally important to him. I personally prefer a small, less expensive economy car, but because my salesmen "respect" bigger cars, I feel that owning a car such as a Continental or a Mercedes builds a better image of me for them.

Your employees will also take pride in contributions you make to your community. I have heard many men and women boast to their friends when local newspapers recognize their employer for making a generous contribution in either money or time to a worthy charity. As with company charitable contributions, when you give to public charities you are demonstrating that your heart is in the right place and that your only interest in not in the "bottom line."

Conclusion

In view of the fact that there are so many facets of business to consider, it is difficult to write a single chapter on the winning image that a company must have with its employees. Perhaps an entire book should be devoted to discussing personnel and public relations, but because of the importance of your relationship with your employees, I would be remiss if I did not include this chapter in *Winning Images*.

5 Going First Class

The obvious connotation of the phrase "going first class" is overspending or extravagance. Perhaps the first thing this expression brings to your mind is a first-class airline ticket, staying at the Plaza rather than at Howard Johnson's, or ordering Chivas Regal instead of the house scotch. In this chapter I will not discuss such obvious examples, but will demonstrate how going first class can, in many cases, build your image to help you accomplish what you are after in a more effective way.

For just a few pennies more, first-class treatment can give you a great deal of extra mileage. A good example is ordering the best-quality business cards your printer can offer. Of course, an attractive business card can be a matter of good taste, so the highest-priced or fanciest is not necessarily the best. What is important, however, is not to pinch pennies by cutting down on the quality of the paper stock used for your cards. If your preference is for the more expensive stock, then by all means order it. Naturally, the same thinking applies to your choice of print. At one thousand cards per order, it probably costs less than a penny for each card, so it's foolish to attempt to economize here. I recommend that you take the same approach to ordering your stationery. In many cases the letter you send to your customer, like the business card the receptionist hands to your prospect in his office, will form his first image of you. The extra penny or two that it costs to have the best is well worthwhile, for you certainly want to have everything going for you at this early stage in the game. When you stop to figure what a company must spend in order for a salesman to give a presentation to a prospect, the expense of high-quality business cards or letterheads is really quite incidental. Many companies have estimated that each presentation to a prospect costs them as much as $50 to $100. When you consider these figures, it is obviously foolish to have your salesmen distribute cheap business cards.

If you go along with the advice to purchase quality stationery and business cards, your next step is to acquire a quality typewriter. Although they are expensive, IBM typewriters, in my opinion, are the best on the market. A clear, crisply typed letter is bound to create a favorable impression on your customers. Typewriters that use carbon ribbon will give your correspondence the best appearance, but if you can't afford these models, always be sure to use a fresh ribbon. By doing so, you will eliminate sloppy or blurred print. For many people, letters are the only tangible means of forming an image of you and your company, so if your letter has a good appearance it will help create the image you desire. A letter with a poor appearance, on the other hand, will give the impression that you either can't afford to go first class or that you simply don't know any better. Because both messages signal that you are a loser, your correspondence will be self-defeating.

If your business requires you to send out formal copies, then another winning-image tip is to use a copy machine that reproduces the original on bond paper. For this, I think the Xerox and IBM copy machines are the best, though, again, they are the most expensive. Both are capable of producing copies that are difficult to distinguish from the original. Such copies will surely make a more favorable impression on your customers than cheap photostats. If you make a lot of copies, using the expensive copiers will cost you only slightly more than the cheaper machines. However, if your use is limited, the cost of the more expensive models may not be warranted. In such case, I suggest you consider using someone else's copying machine or employing a copying service.

You must also keep in mind the importance of well-written letters. If they are especially important, write them with extreme care, revising them as much as is necessary to convey your message in a coherent, concise, and clear manner. If English wasn't one of your strong subjects in school, hire a good secretary who can be responsible for correcting or rewording your letters.

Just as the above-mentioned items build a good image in your communication with your customers, so do many other items that you carry with you to your customer's office. For example, a first-class briefcase may initially cost you more money, but it creates a very effective image. You should look for this same high quality in a fountain pen or a pocket calculator. Such possessions can and do build an image of you, and the image should never be less than a favorable one. I have had many salesmen call on me with ripped briefcases (which sometimes don't even open), calculators that don't work, and cheap pens that won't write. The impression these items created in me—and I think this is true for most people—is that both the salesman and his company are neither professional nor successful. In our highly competitive society, people like to deal with successful people because they feel these people must be good at what they do. Consequently it is essential that you buy first-class, professional tools so that you can create a winning image. As we all know, "a mechanic is only as good as his tools" —especially since quality products cost only a few pennies more in the long run, and perhaps are even less expensive.

As I mentioned in the chapter on appearances and first impressions, the manner in which you dress is one of the best image-builders of all. I would, as I said there, prefer to own two fine-quality suits rather than a wardrobe of twenty cheap ones. There's no reason why the vast majority of the people who read this book cannot afford to shop at the better clothing stores. If your taste in clothes is poor, I recommend that you seek the advice of a good dresser who can help you coordinate your wardrobe. This is especially important for those of you who deal with the public on a daily basis, as does the salesman, retailer, business executive, attorney, accountant, architect, and TV personality.

One of my strongest pet peeves is the wearing of cheap toupees because nothing—absolutely nothing— looks worse. A bald man will have a better image than the man who wears a poorly made hairpiece. Women can heed the same advice concerning wigs. If you're going to wear a hairpiece, wear a good one.

If you can afford it, a prestigious office building,

rather than a cheap one in a lower-priced neighborhood, will create a better image for your business. Professional men such as attorneys, CPAs, architects, and life insurance agents must have first-class offices if they expect to cater to first-class clients. I also recommend that you employ the services of an interior decorator in coordinating your offices. If you don't feel you can afford one, perhaps you should reconsider, because this is an important business investment. After all, professionals do not purchase equipment or inventories; so, as service businesses, their overhead is really very low in comparison with that of other companies. When you do decorate, don't go overboard and definitely avoid being gaudy. If you shun interior decorators because you heard they are expensive or because you think they are likely to be too fancy, you are doing yourself a disservice in terms of your image. The vast majority of corporate executives use good decorators to help them create the image they are after.

If money is no object, there is no limit to what you can spend in decorating your office. You can start by purchasing the finest furniture, carpeting your floors with oriental rugs, and decorating your walls with original paintings. And if you can't afford Picasso's paintings, you can settle for lithographs or prints of his and other fine artists' work.

Other good-image builders for your office walls are those that "tell a story." Used by many executives, such tell-a-story image-builders include certificates, diplomas, and achievement and recognition awards. Of course, there are also the photographs of your family, and there's nothing wrong in creating the family-man image. Besides, these pictures cover up blank walls!

I know one particular life insurance agent who arranges for his clients to visit him in his office whenever possible. He tries to establish the same kind of relationship with his clients that an attorney does with his. Although working from his own office allows him to have more information available at his fingertips when planning a client's program, the main reason he does so is strictly for image-building purposes. His offices are exquisitely furnished, and on his walls are the many awards he has received, including Phi Beta Kappa, Life Member of the Million Dollar Round Table, Chartered Life Underwriter, college diplomas, dozens of plaques that designate him as one of his company's sales leaders, and others that recognize him for outstanding achievements in community work. His interview-in-his-office technique of doing business is highly effective because, as he explains, "I am not interrupted in my own office as my client is in his, and, consequently, he does not lose his trend of thought when he is here. (I like a captive office!) Secondly, my walls give him a special message about who I am that he could not get if I went to his office—besides, isn't the home court worth an extra six points?"

Before we leave our discussion about the office, I strongly urge you to hire a first-class secretary. You'll definitely get your money's worth from her, and you shouldn't hesitate to spend more because her services will certainly be worth it. A secretary who expertly answers the phone, takes your calls, handles people in the reception room, takes dictation, types, and files is essential to the well-being of the business. This is a very poor area in which to cut corners. You should also apply the same thinking when hiring other people for your office.

Having the best and most prestigious attorneys and CPA firms represent you is also very valuable. When you mention the name of the best law firm in town while discussing a contract you are negotiating with a prospective client, not only do you carry more weight, but you also help your company's image. Letting outsiders know that your company is audited by such highly respected firms as Arthur Andersen, Coopers and Lybrand, or Peat, Marwick, Mitchell, and Company (or any of the other Big Eight accounting firms) is always beneficial in terms of your image. You get what you pay for when you go to the best, and first-class professional services are not only important image-builders, but also very necessary in the long-range performance of your business.

There are other ways of going first class that are expensive, but if you can afford them, they are worth the cost. For example, professional men in real estate, insurance, stock brokerage, securities, legal accounting, and architecture are always endeavoring to attract new clients who are successful. These men must mingle with people who have higher incomes so that they can establish their practice. Such "selling" often involves joining country clubs and living in the best neighborhood in town. While it might seem insincere to tie your private and social life to your business, until you establish a reputation that draws people to you, you're going to have to rub shoulders with such persons in order to build up a thriving practice. I once asked a good friend of mine, who has a successful law firm, why he belonged to both a country and a city club when he didn't drink or play golf. His answer was, "Bob, as Willie Sutton said when they asked him why he robbed banks, 'Because that's where the money is.'" He added, "Even though I don't use their facilities, the clubs are always great image-builders, not only for entertaining but also for making contacts."

You should always go first class when you entertain your business associates. It only costs a few dollars more to dine at the really fine restaurants or drink

"And most importantly, it's great for your image."

good liquor. Never pinch pennies when you entertain a client. At the same time, don't be obnoxious by
obviously trying to impress him. Let him choose what
he wants; don't insist that he order the most expensive
item on the menu. If he does inquire about the special-
ity of the house, however, it's perfectly all right to
make a recommendation. When entertaining at home,
quality is again the magic word. If you are entertaining
a group of twelve or more, it's a good idea to engage a professional bartender to serve drinks. Otherwise, you will spend all your own time serving your
guests rather than enjoying the party. The bartender's
fee will probably be less than what the liquor would
cost if the guests serve themselves. So, not only do his
services add more class to your party, they are practical as well.

Also follow the important rule of always picking
up the tab at lunch. Next to buying first-class business
cards, the cheapest investment you can make in terms
of building your image is to buy someone a lunch.
Your time has little or no value if you can't afford to
pay for this meal, because at a business lunch, the
most expensive thing being consumed is your time.

Conclusion

Going first class is a matter of course for many well-
to-do people. It is also the style the man on his way
up must emulate. There are good ways of going first
class that have not been discussed in this chapter,
ranging from giving important clients color TV sets to
owning a yacht or even flying a Lear jet. Depending
on your market and what you are attempting to accomplish, these luxuries may sometimes be just the

first-class tickets you need to get things done. For most readers of this book, these first-class image-builders are way out of reach, but there are many other means available to you for creating the image you seek.

The Stability Principle

In most of your relationships, you'll find that the people you deal with are interested in the long-range picture. The exceptions are those you meet on those occasional one-night stands (and you can't really concern yourself with your image for them). Since your clients, customers, co-workers, and business associates are the people who really count, following what I call the "Stability Principle" can be very valuable in helping you build a winning image for both them and yourself. People need to know that their relationships with you are durable. Everyone realizes that flash-in-the-pan types cannot be counted on, and such an image scares people away. Because banks and insurance companies realized this principle long ago, they constructed giant edifices to tell their customers that they had stability.

Take a good look around the next time you visit the bank and you will see what I am talking about. Every bank seeks a certain traditional look that conveys to its customers a feeling of permanency. You will notice this same characteristic if you ever visit the home office building of an insurance company. If people are going to put their lifetime savings in banks or invest in life insurance policies, they need to believe that those institutions will "live forever." They want to be assured that their heirs will receive that to which they are entitled. The image insurance companies and banks employ is one that makes people believe that nothing is more permanent than a solidly constructed office building. Such a building towers over the rest of the community, and there is never any fear that someday it won't be there. Some banks and insurance companies get the same message across to the public in a different way. Instead of owning their own property, they become major tenants in large office buildings. Yet because they place their name on the top of the building, most people believe they own it. I know of some companies that have taken less than 10 percent of the floor space in a forty- or fifty-story building, but have had their names either posted on the top of the building or engraved in the concrete or marble walls of the entrance.

When you visit smaller towns, you will generally find that the two handsomest buildings are the local bank and the funeral home. Because a grieved family needs stability during its period of sorrow, funeral home directors are also concerned with conveying this image. Of course, you will notice that churches and synagogues are also monuments and they exist for the same reason—the stability principle.

In my own business I realized the importance of this principle in image-building many years ago, and when the timing was right, I built my own office building, which still houses my executive headquarters in Colum-

bus, Ohio. Even though I could just as easily have leased space, I felt that owning a building would give my customers a better sense of security. It represents a long-term image, one people believe will be around for many years after they are gone. This same sense of security is also created among my business associates, which is important in terms of building good business relationships. Naturally, the "right" piece of real estate is also a worthwhile investment, but it is essential that you carefully evaluate the economics involved before making any purchase so that you might build a better image.

Owning a permanent fixture is even more important for a service type of business than for businesses that have fixed assets in their equipment or carry large inventories. Because its very nature is intangible, a service business has a greater need for the Stability Principle. This kind of business requires something concrete to see and touch—which it doesn't have with its product.

There are many ways of incorporating the Stability Principle without going to the expense of acquiring a large piece of real estate. Since an office building must be located in one place, only the local people will ever see it. How much value does your salesman in Kansas City derive from the high-rise office building in downtown Philadelphia that bears the name of your company? Many smaller, less expensive image-builders are available for the Kansas City representative to use, and they can also be very helpful to you in establishing the right image. Since nothing gives a company a weaker image than handmade sales aids or makeshift sales kits, I am a firm believer in first-class sales aids for all salesmen. Without them, prospective clientele suspect the company lacks both professionalism and money, or assume that it is new in its field. Any of these poor images will definitely decrease the company's chances of achieving its share of the market.

The use of advertising specialties bearing the company's name is also important in image-building. Pocket knives, diaries, briefcases, desk sets, or any other items of a tangible, long-lasting nature will suggest to your clients that you have stability. Unlike what you tell him about your company, these giveaways are something concrete that your prospect can hold in his hand.

The salesman has to confront a widespread attitude among customers, which is: "Sure, the salesmen are always around when it is time to sell to me, but they never seem to be around when I need the service." You must engender in potential customers a sense of trust in the stability of your salesmen in order to create a winning image for your company.

With new and smaller-sized older businesses, the stability image is more difficult to project, but it can be done. And these are the companies that need it the most! When my father and I first started our company, recruiting new salesmen was difficult because we were competing head-on with giant insurance companies that had well-established stability images. As a small father-son insurance agency operating out of the basement of a residence (incidentally, we never referred to it as the basement, but as the "lower level"), we had to take a different approach because we realized that we couldn't directly tackle companies like Prudential or Metropolitan. What we did instead was to play up our "expertise" as professional salesmen and offer personalized training and development programs to new salesmen—something that the "biggies" couldn't do. Building up our own image as experts was important because *we* were the only tangible thing we had to offer!

On many occasions a new recruit would ask, "What kind of future can your company offer me? How can I be sure that you'll be in business five years from now?" I heard these questions so often that I began to hear them in my sleep! The only response we had for such inquiries was to say, "Every major company started out basically the same way we are. If you aren't smart enough to recognize an opportunity that's still on the ground floor, then you aren't the man we're looking for." Sometimes this answer worked; many times it didn't. Yet this is just part of the game you must accept if you're starting a new business. Since the only thing we had to sell was ourselves, the winning image we strove for was one of integrity, motivation, and sincerity. These were our chief assets because we had no tangible ones to display.

As we grew, and after we had a few years behind us, we were able to demonstrate certain successes as well as boast an excellent track record, which, for a company of our size, was achieved in a very short period of time. Naturally, as we grew older, we could tell the world that we had been in business since 1961. We were as old as Xerox! Perhaps thirty years from now we'll put on our stationery and on the entrance of our building: Founded in 1961. It's amazing how many companies have nothing to say about themselves except how old they are. If that's all they've got, they should flaunt it because it will impress many people!

After we were in business for a few years, we had an attractive brochure printed about our company, and we distributed copies to new salesmen. This brochure told about our successes and was an effective means of giving a new man something tangible to take home to his wife. When she asked about us, he could not only tell her, but show her as well. My father and I also gave a free autographed copy of our book to

all prospective salesmen to take home after the first
interview. We wanted them to have something of sub-
stance to see and hold, and presenting them with the
book (which retailed for $9.95) was well worth the
cost of increasing our effectiveness in recruiting new
sales people. As an image-builder, the book gave us
added stability in the salesmen's eyes because if you
write about your profession, you're supposedly an expert. We actually are, but not everybody believed it
until we had the book to prove it!

Not everybody has the time or the aptitude to write
a book and get it published, so perhaps this kind of
image-building is an exception to the rule. Nevertheless, there are many other practical ways by which you
can create an image of stability. One of the least expensive, as mentioned earlier, is to be concerned with
your appearance—particularly with the way you dress.

The Stability Principle is especially important for
companies on their way up. As they grow larger and
older, they place less emphasis on this image because they become so well known that their stability
is no longer a question. An individual who becomes
highly successful and acquires a great deal of wealth
also reaches a point where he wants to reverse his role
and become what we call the "old-shoe" type. How
many times have you seen an extremely wealthy person drive an old, inexpensive car, wear casual, out-
of-date clothes, and, in short, do the opposite of what
rich people are expected to do? I believe that the I-
don't-care attitude such people cultivate builds even
more stability into their image. Other people interpret
their attitude toward material things to mean that the
successful individual no longer has to concern himself
with what less successful people consider status symbols.

The nouveaux riches, on the other hand, shake the

confidence of those around them because they spend their money as if it's going out of style. In many cases their spending habits are in poor taste and are resented by others. People begin to think, "Tom Katz has become too impressed with his money. He's no longer capable of concentrating on his work, and he'll soon lose both his business and his money."

While I don't mean to overemphasize the Stability Principle, its importance requires that we consider it in all its manifestations. If you've ever noticed how children who are being reprimanded react to their parents, you know that they want to be disciplined. For an executive, unless he adheres to the Stability Principle and does not try to be Mr. Nice Guy, he will not be effective in his dealings with his associates. Whenever necessary, you must lay down the law and be firm with people. If disciplinary action is in order, you must follow it through, even if doing so makes you feel like an SOB. Your employee may not like you for it, but he'll respect you because he'd be disappointed if you failed to correct a wrong. In selling, this is particularly true of customers, who aren't accustomed to being treated with firmness. The respect you gain from them gives you added control of the sale. Ruby Diamond, a top men's sportswear salesman, will tell a customer who doesn't give him a large enough order, "Look, Jack, I can't turn in such a small order to my company. If I did, they would take away your exclusivity in this area. Now let's go over this order once again, and see if we can't increase it."

When you're right, you must deal with people firmly. Proceeding on this basis is one of the main ways of developing the maximum effectiveness of the Stability Principle in your relationships with customers, employees, and business associates on every level.

Several years ago I was compelled to be firm and

assertive with a funeral director, an older, impatient man, who insisted on rushing me through my sales presentation and asking me how much the premium was going to cost for someone his age. Finally, I answered him by saying, "Look, Mr. Strange, for the past ten minutes you haven't listened to a thing I said. All you want to know is how much premium you have to pay. You have absolutely no idea of what you're going to get in return for your money. Now what I'm going to have to do is start from the very beginning and tell you all over what you don't know because you weren't listening. Because I won't do it again, listen carefully this time." When I finished, I expected either to get thrown out or to have a very quiet and captive audience. Mr. Strange didn't say a word, and I had an easy sale once I was finally able to show him the premium. He respected me for treating him with firmness, and if I had not done so, I would have lost a sale.

Conclusion

In all facets of life, the Stability Principle can greatly affect your relationship with others. Although *Winning Images* is primarily devoted to careers, you can undoubtedly see that the Stability Principle can also be of vital importance in building your personal image as a father, mother, husband, or wife. As a matter of fact, a family must have this image in order to function harmoniously.

On a larger scale, a politician must convey an image of stability to the voter, and on a still larger scale, all levels of government must do the same in order to gain the support and confidence of the people. Once you remove the stability image from government, the entire nation may crumble.

7 The Credibility Principle

We will now discuss the "Credibility Principle": *Do whatever you say you are going to do*. Though simple and rational, this principle is not followed by the vast majority of people. The person who does what he says he will do is a rare individual who stands tall in the crowd.

Certainly we've all been in situations where we were "promised" performance and received only disappointment. I am not necessarily talking about the promise of success that didn't materialize, but the hassle that resulted from a failure to meet a "guaranteed" deadline or a performance projection that was grossly overstated. At one time or another all of us have shared the frustration that followed the unfulfilled promise: "My check is in the mail." How many times have you been disappointed when a tailor failed to have your suit or dress altered by the promised date? Perhaps a computer salesman "guaranteed" you delivery of the

7000 Model by the 25th of the month, but you didn't receive it until two weeks later. Remember when the contractor assured you that your swimming pool would be completed no later than June 10, but you weren't able to take your first swim until September 2? How about the time you were promised your new car by the first of the month but didn't receive it until almost four weeks past the scheduled date? All of us have suffered these kinds of frustrations and agonized over such broken promises. The failure to perform as promised is a losing image, and you must avoid it like the plague.

Dwight Knight, a very bright attorney with a leading law firm in town, is a perfect example of someone who violates the Credibility Principle. In spite of his outstanding ability as a corporate lawyer, his constant failure to meet promised deadlines causes him to lose much if not all of the goodwill he creates by his ability to "put out a good product." "Why, sure," Dwight tells his client, "I'll have the final contracts drawn up by Wednesday. I see absolutely no reason whatsoever for any delay. What time do you want them? Will the morning around tenish be all right?"

In view of Dwight's past performance record, it's always advisable to call him prior to sending a secretary over to pick up the contract. Chances are that when you do, his receptionist will say, "Oh, Mr. Knight is tied up in conference until noon. May he return your call after he's back from lunch?" Toward the end of the day, when you still haven't heard from him, you will give him a call before you leave the office, but he's still going to be unavailable. On Thursday, the day after the scheduled appointment, he gives you the run-around for the entire day! By Friday you're fit to be tied, and when he finally does allow you to be put through on the phone, he meekly mumbles, "You know, those contracts are really much more complicated than first meets the eye. Why, I had no idea they were going to be so difficult. There's so much more involved than I had imagined." As he hems and haws, there is no possible explanation he can give you that will be acceptable—*he failed to meet the deadline.* Since you know he's not incompetent, you can only conclude that he just doesn't give a damn whether he inconveniences you or not! Although you may be locked into working with him on this particular contract, your mind swiftly begins to think about replacing his law firm with another one.

Attorneys aren't the only professionals who cause this kind of unnecessary frustration for their clients. Doctors are just as guilty. My "ex" personal physician, Boris Morris, almost made me mad enough to give him a black eye for the abuse he inflicted upon me. I was required to get a physical examination for a large life insurance policy I had applied for, so I had my secretary set up an appointment with Dr. Morris for the first thing in the morning. "Tell him to be at the office at eight-thirty," the nurse told my secretary, "and we'll have Mr. Shook in and out in no time flat!" I arrived at the doctor's office ten minutes before it opened, and, much to my dismay, twenty other patients were also waiting in the reception room when the nurse arrived at twenty to nine to open the door to let everyone in. Dr. Morris came in through his private back-door entrance at ten after nine, and at ten-thirty I was finally asked to fill out a form. At eleven, I was led into a small room and told to take off my shirt. Like a fool, I stood in this stark examining room for fifteen minutes before the good doctor finally burst through the door and said, "And how is my good friend, Bob Shook, this morning?"

I won't go into detail about what I answered, but I

will say that there was absolutely no reason in the
world for his lack of consideration. He had inconven-
ienced me and twenty other people by telling us all
to be at his office at the same early hour. This is just
plain disrespect for others' time, and no one has a
right to treat anyone so rudely. I understand there are
many doctors who display this kind of contempt for
their patients, and they continue to conduct their practices in this way, even though several people tell them
that doing so is inexcusable.

Perhaps the most infamous individuals who make
promises that they don't fulfill are politicians. It's a sad
commentary on our political system and a distasteful
fact of life that the average American has lost confidence in our local and national leadership. This loss of
confidence can be a much greater problem than first
meets the eye because widespread mistrust in our government can cause the downfall of our free enterprise
system. Campaign promises are too often made in an
attempt to win votes, not with the intention of actual
performance. This is probably the most notorious situation in which the public *expects* promises to be broken.

I believe in respecting the next man, and when I
tell him that he can count on something, I do it without
fail according to schedule. I don't care if I have to
stay up for two nights; I'll meet my deadline, barring
an unforeseeable accident or illness. To date, I have
been blessed with excellent health and have only had
to miss one day's work in the last fifteen years because
of sickness. Even now, because I have a deadline to
meet with my publisher, I am writing this chapter in
my office on a Sunday morning at six-fifteen because
I *will* definitely be on schedule!

Keeping commitments was very important to us
when my father and I started our business, and to this

day that is still a high priority. In the beginning we realized how important it was for us to establish credibility with the various insurance companies our agency represented. Consequently, we vowed to always obey the Credibility Principle to the letter. We realized that the very nature of most salesmen is to oversell and never do quite what they say they will. Hence, we felt that giving these companies slightly lower figures than we actually anticipated in sales volume for the upcoming year was preferable to quoting higher figures. At the year's end they were then pleasantly surprised by the "extra" business they received. Even though they would have received the same amount of sales volume regardless of the projections, we felt it was better to give them more than they expected rather than to *disappoint them by giving them less.* Many times throughout the years we have been told, "You people are the only sales organization in the entire industry who actually meet the production figure you give. In most cases, we simply cut the predictions in half and come up with a reasonable estimate of what an agency will actually do."

Everybody has dealt with people who constantly stretch the facts when they project what they're going to do. What is amazing is that such people do not have the foresight to see how foolish they are going to appear when they fail to produce what they have promised. In our company, for example, we ask each salesman to give us a twelve-month projection of the volume he expects to produce during the upcoming year. If we were to total the amounts of these projections and then actually hit those annual figures, we would be in a position to retire! In many cases a salesman's projections are so unrealistic that he gets too far behind by April and must therefore disregard his sales goals and establish more realistic ones for the rest of the year.

If there is a "best" time to give accurate projections, I would suggest that it is when you visit your banker for a loan. Never, absolutely never, give your banker inflated projections unless you are positive you will meet them. In fact, I have found that it's always better to give him slightly lower projections so when the end of your fiscal year arrives, you can present him with better figures than he was expecting. If you're going to surprise a banker, do it with good news, not bad!

Since a good relationship with their bank(s) is highly essential for most businesses, credibility must be established early in the game. The majority of businesses ignore the Credibility Principle, and in their zest to make a good impression on a loan officer, they *oversell*. While they may think they're making a good impression, they're actually making a foolish mistake, because six months, a year, even three years go by so quickly, and the banker won't forget what was projected. He's written it all down and presented the financial forecasts to his bank examiner. If the business fails to meet projections, he's going to want a full explanation of *why* the forecast was off, and it's going to be difficult to talk to him. Doesn't it make good sense to project less than what you're relatively certain you can do, and then surprise him with the good news of having done even better? After all, you're planning to do business with your banker for a long period of time, so don't place doubt in his mind that will cause him to think, "Well, if he's asking for this figure, we'll just cut it in half."

We like to believe that others are going to follow through when we deal with them, but many simply will not. I know several highly talented men and women who do not follow through, and as a result they frustrate everyone who deals with them, causing many to decide never to do business with them again. Lynn Flynn, a real estate agent, is a good example of an excellent salesperson, who, though she has all the talent necessary to do a fine job, lacks the commitment to follow through on what she initially tackles. Clark Barr, a friend of mine who was transferred to our city from out of town a few years ago, told me about the exhausting experience he had when he and his wife Gay were house-hunting. "Bob, I never saw anything like it in my life," he said. "I had to get a house because we sold our home in Michigan, and we only had sixty days before we had to vacate it so the buyers could move in. I explained all this to Lynn and she told me that she had dozens of homes like the one we were looking for, and no broker in town had as many exclusive listings. Well, Gay and I couldn't get over it," he continued. "No matter how many times we called her, she stalled us and gave excuses about why this house or that house wouldn't be suitable. One day, my wife saw *the* dream home and it had a For Sale sign in front. When Gay called Lynn to ask for a showing, she told us that she had just sold it to some other family the day before. We were so mad that we decided to contact Holmes Realty and do you know what? We ended up buying a ninety-thousand-dollar home from them within five days. I'll bet Gay has sent Holmes at least eight other customers who've also been transferred here by our company. I know for a fact that I've told at least a dozen more to stay away from Lynn Flynn! She's a nice gal, but it's just plain murder to deal with somebody like that."

Unfortunately, all of us have dealt with people like Lynn Flynn at one time or another, and when we do, we learn to appreciate the *professional* who does what

The credibility gap.

he says he will. Life is simply too short to go through the same exasperating situation twice with the person who let you down because he didn't deliver the goods as originally promised. Many people whose talent borders on genius achieve only mediocre results in their career because they lack the necessary follow-through to actually perform well. Less gifted people continually outperform these so-called geniuses because they come through when they're supposed to. No matter how outstanding the end result may be, you do not receive *full value for services rendered* if you suffer unbearable frustrations because *the other person didn't do what he said he would do according to schedule.*

Conclusion

If it is your intention to build a long and rewarding career, you must plan to do business with others over a long period of time. Your output, plus your ability to apply the Credibility Principle, will determine your success in the long run. This is the winning image you must develop if your career is to enjoy longevity.

Success Breeds Success

As the saying goes, nothing succeeds like success. People like to deal with a successful person. Why? Because there must be a reason why this person has achieved success, and the most obvious reason is that he is good at what he does. When given a choice, people want to deal with the best.

Naturally, the very best way to create a success image is to do outstanding work. Your performance, and the reputation it creates, will inform the public of how good you really are. People will know this by your previous track record or simply by recognizing it upon seeing you in action. Just as it becomes quite obvious that a man is a professional tennis player when you see him play on the court, so will it become obvious that you are professional in your field when people see you perform. But many other image-building techniques are applicable in creating a success image, and these are the techniques that will be discussed in this chapter.

Here we are not concerned with flamboyant ways to build your image, such as driving a big car, buying a home you can't afford, belonging to country clubs that are beyond your budget, or employing any other four-flushing trick that is not within your means. The winning-image-building techniques that follow are subtle and low key.

We can agree, I think, that everybody likes to deal with successful people who are winners. The more successful they are, the more business they will do because success does breed success. A recent experience I had with my dentist is a good illustration of this point. As I was on my way out of his office after getting my semi-annual checkup, his receptionist asked me if I would be available for another examination on June 23. Surprised, I replied, "Why next month? I thought I just received a clean bill of health and it wouldn't be necessary for me to come back for another six months." She laughed and said, "Mr. Shook, I'm not talking about next month. We're completely booked up through June of *next year*." I quickly answered, "In that case, you'd better put me down because if I don't give you a date now, I'll probably have to wait even longer!" Learning that my dentist was booked thirteen months in advance impressed me a great deal. His flourishing practice assured me that I must have the best dentist in town.

Another experience I had with a dentist several years ago did not give me this same assurance. When I called to make an appointment, he told me he could see me the next morning at nine. Since I wouldn't be able to make it at that time, he agreed to give me an eleven o'clock appointment, but after I checked my own schedule I saw that I couldn't make it then, either.

Finally, he consented to see me at ten. My immediate
reaction to our conversation was to think that the poor
guy had no patients from nine to twelve on that particular day. I figured that any dentist who was not
solidly booked up for the following day must not have
a thriving practice. Although I did keep the appointment, I was quite apprehensive about what kind of
work he was capable of doing, since he did not seem
to be in demand. As you can see, he created a very
poor image, and once such a bad one is formed, he has
two strikes against him in establishing the necessary
confidence his patients must have in him.

If your business is new, or if it has been in progress
for several years but has not yet reached a satisfac-
tory level, I strongly recommend that you closely adhere to the Success-Breeds-Success Principle. The first
lesson you should learn is always to *appear busy*.
Never let your clients know how few appointments
you may have; instead, create the impression that you
are "solidly booked."

Whenever a prospect was not available to see me at
a certain time, I would always say something like,
"Fred, I'm sorry we can't meet on Tuesday morning at
eight, but I can see you on Friday afternoon at two-
fifteen or next Tuesday morning at nine-thirty." I may
not have had one single appointment for the next two
months, but when I pulled out my appointment book
and busily thumbed through it, my prospect got the
impression that I had a busy schedule. More than
likely, he felt fortunate to be able to see me on those
dates I suggested.

Occasionally, however, a prospect would say,
"Sorry, Bob, I'm booked up on those dates, but I could
see you on Thursday at two." If I didn't tell him that
I couldn't make it and give him another date, I would
say, "Fine. I'm sure I can do some schedule-juggling

in order to see you then. Please be sure to mark it down on your own calendar because mine is very tight!" Although I did not say it in these words, my message was quite clear: *I am very successful, and therefore I am very busy.*

As mentioned in the chapter "The Starting-a-New-Business Image," my plastic surgeon friend obviously got an A on his thesis, "The Success-Breeds-Success Principle." Never in a million years would he tell the parents of a prospective patient, "Look, folks, I will be glad to give her a new nose any time you want to bring her in during the next three weeks. Since I have nothing on my agenda, you name the time and I will be available." Would you entrust the future beauty of your daughter to such a doctor?

One of the best examples of the success-breeds-success technique is the professional man who actually does you a *big* favor by allowing you to be his client or patient. Doctors who have so-called closed practices are telling the public that they have all the patients they can handle, and therefore all others must be put on a waiting list. They are not, however, the only ones who close their practices. I know of many interior decorators who only *sometimes* give you the honor of paying them for their services if you're not already a client. I also know a few Wall Street stockbrokers who practically run a financial report on you before they'll permit you to give them your money to invest. These people are masterful at using the success-breeds-success image.

Appearing to be busy is especially important for smaller businesses. I am always amused at how such firms will put their customers through a thorough cross-examination before allowing them to speak with the "top dog." After you go through a detailed explanation of who you are and why you are calling to the girl who answers the phone, she will transfer your call to her employer's private secretary. The secretary will ask you the same questions again. By the time you get to speak with whomever you called, you've spoken to just about everybody in the office. Yet this technique does create an air of importance. Many people believe that the more receptionists and secretaries they must talk to in order to reach the party they're calling, the more important he must be. Although it's very acceptable for a really big executive to answer the phone personally, the small businessman who answers the phone himself creates an image of operating a small business. It is usually true that really small businessmen rarely have receptionists or secretaries to protect them.

A second winning-image technique of the Success-Breeds-Success Principle is to have a successful-looking appearance. If your shirt collar is frayed, your shoes not shined, your lapels out of style, or your tie unclean, you are evidently either unsuccessful and can't afford to dress properly, or you're just a slob! With either of these images, you're definitely a loser.

Appearances were discussed in Chapter 3, but it cannot be overemphasized that the appearance of your office building, its decor, and its equipment are important. Although the rent might be higher in a luxurious, high-rise, downtown office building than in a one-floor, converted storeroom in a low-rent district, the extra rental may be the best bargain you ever make.

The Success-Breeds-Success Principle suggests that you decorate your office walls with symbols that enhance your image. Diplomas, certificates of academic degrees and the like are very effective in telling your prospect just how good you really are. So are any plaques and awards you have received. A friend of mine who is a prominent attorney decorated his office

"I'm sorry, but he's in conference right now."

with beautifully framed eight-by-ten photographs of himself and different board members sitting around conference tables. Since he serves on many of his major clients' boards of directors, people sooner or later either recognize a prominent businessman in one of the pictures or ask what the photographs represent. Such a leading question allows him to give his "spiel" about the companies on whose boards he serves (who says lawyers aren't allowed to advertise?). His pictures are very impressive, and I can't help thinking that he must be very proud of such recognition. He must also be very good if he serves as a member of these companies' boards.

The success-breeds-success image is undoubtedly the most significant reason why many people in the arts are able to demand such high prices for their work. The artist, for example, who establishes the reputation of being expensive soon gets more for his work than many unknown artists who have as much or even more talent. Again, the secret is in his ability *to build a winning image,* not in his talent to paint on canvas. How many times have you seen a piece of modern art that resembles the work of a grade-school student but costs three times your annual salary, even though it may have taken the artist only an hour to produce? The most amazing thing about such art is that people actually buy it and then resell it at a high profit.

It's human nature to feel at times that the more you pay for services, the higher the quality of the work you receive. Most people think, "At those prices, I've got the best that money can buy." I can remember a house painter who gave us an estimate less than half the price of the painting contractor who was supposedly the best in town. Instead of jumping for his services, my wife automatically became "gun-shy" and didn't want to use him. "What kind of work can he do at such low prices?" she asked. Although I was going to supply the finest paint, she insisted, "His work will probably last for only a third of the time, so we'll be better off in the long run if we pay the top price now." I must admit that there is much to be said in favor of equating quality with the price tag of merchandise. For this reason it's very important to price your services high enough so that you don't scare people away.

Doctors, attorneys, business consultants, accountants, dentists, or anyone else who must charge a fee for services rendered should very carefully analyze the fee schedule he or she decides to use. As pointed out, you can create a negative image by charging fees that are too low, and doing so will damage your practice, for you will do less business. Raising your fees to the price that makes you *look expensive* suggests that you *are also good!*

Since the Success-Breeds-Success Principle is a means of advertising how good you really are, it also applies to publications concerning your company's service. An expensive but effective technique of image-building is for a regional company to advertise in a national magazine, but on a *regional basis*. Most people are not aware of the fact that national publications such as the *Wall Street Journal, Business Week, Fortune, Forbes, Time,* and *Newsweek* have lower rates for advertisements that appear only in magazines distributed in a particular section of the country. The average reader who sees such ads concludes, "Wow, I didn't realize that Columbus Widget Company is doing such a big job. Since they took a full-page ad in *Time* magazine, business must really be booming!" For companies doing business on a regional basis, ads of this type can be very worthwhile. When advertising in this manner, however, be certain you don't pay for reaching a market so large you're incapable of servicing it.

Conclusion

Perhaps a friend of mine summed up the Success-Breeds-Success Principle best when he confided to me: "You know, Bob, before I was successful, I used to make the same profound statements I make now, but nobody ever listened. As a matter of fact, they even used to laugh at some of my far-out ideas. Now they listen to me. And the very same people who used to practically ignore what I had to say are the ones who always agree with me now."

Excelling in your work is essential, but employing the Success-Breeds-Success Principle guarantees that you will obtain the image you seek. People want to deal with other people who are successful because they believe that those who have succeeded must be good at what they do, or they wouldn't have achieved their present status. In order to be the best, you must show the public that you really are.

The Brand-Name Image

Once the brand-name image is established, it's worth its weight in gold. A well-accepted quality product with a winning image occupies a very advantageous position. Such a position is difficult to get, but when you stop to consider its value, striving to obtain it is certainly worthwhile.

Suppose, for instance, you are about to purchase a new television set. You are shopping at a typical discount store, and you have narrowed your choice down to two seemingly identical sets. As you turn them on, the picture in both seems to be exactly alike. In fact, you detect no difference except that the cost of one is $450 and the cost of the other only $400. The more expensive set is an RCA and the less expensive set is called a Corona. How many people, including yourself, will decide to save $50 by taking a chance on the Corona? Quite frankly, as much as I like to get a bargain,

I know darn well I would purchase the RCA. That's the advantage of a brand-name image!

The same lesson can be applied to any product. Imagine that you are shopping for a new suit. Again, you have narrowed your choice to two suits. Each appears to be of the same quality. One suit is a Hart, Shaffner, Marx and the other is an H. Weeman. Would you be willing to save 25 percent by purchasing the H. Weeman suit? "Why, it will probably last only a third as long," thinks the average buyer. "In the long run, I'll get a much better value if I purchase the Hart, Shaffner, Marx suit." Since he believes he has made a wise choice, such a customer will walk out of the store feeling quite satisfied with both his purchase and himself.

After I graduated from college and began my sales career, I was offered a sales position by a New York manufacturer of straw hats. When I visited the plant, I was given the grand tour. Upon being shown through the warehouse, I noticed a large shipment of boxes addressed to Rivers Bros., and commented to the owner of the company, "You do quite a large business with Rivers Brothers, Harry. I didn't realize that they carried Wallbanger Hats."

"Yes, they do," Harry replied, "but because they put the Rivers Brothers label in the hats, nobody knows they're Wallbangers."

As we walked further down the corridor of the large warehouse, I noticed what seemed to be thousands of hats being sent out to Burns. I said, "I notice that you also do quite a large business with Burns. I'm very impressed."

"That's right." He smiled. "Burns does a big job with the exact same hat we ship to Rivers Brothers."

When I took a hat out of each store's hat box, I exclaimed, "Aw, come on, you're putting me on. These can't possibly be the same hat. But, boy, do they ever look alike."

Harry laughed and said, "Since you're such an expert on hats, Bob, how about telling me what's different about each of them."

I carefully examined the two hats, tried them on, squeezed them, and even smelled them (although to this day I don't know why I smelled them). "I give up," I said. "I know there's got to be a difference, but I guess I'm too green in the hat business to be able to tell. What is the big difference?"

Harry threw back his head and howled. "Bob, they're absolutely identical except for two things: they've got different labels on the inside and different price tags. The Burns hat retails for thirty-three and a third percent less than the Rivers Brothers hat." The thing that really shocked me was what he said next. "Even though the two hats are identical, there's a certain type of Madison Avenue customer, fresh out of some Ivy League school, who could not be convinced, even by me, that the two hats are exactly the same. He'll try both hats on, and he'll tell you that the Rivers hat is more comfortable. He'll swear that the straw in the more expensive hat is of better quality. And he'll tell me, who has been in the business of manufacturing Wallbanger Hats for thirty years, that the cheaper hat will undoubtedly fall apart after having been worn only a few times!"

I became a strong believer in the power of a brand-name image as I walked through the warehouse of Wallbanger Hats for the reason that, deep down, I knew that I, too, would have spent a few extra dollars to purchase the Rivers Bros. hat. When I left the hat-manufacturing plant, I stopped to buy gasoline at an off-brand service station. Though I had heard for years that major brand-name stations and off-brand stations all used the same gas from the same tanks, this was the first time in my life that I had ever gone to an off-brand service station.

One more classic example will show you how even the so-called experts go for the brand-name image. Recently, at our company management meeting, we were discussing the possibility of replacing our group Blue Cross insurance plan with something less expensive, since our rates had been hiked by 50 percent during the previous month. One of my associates from Georgia presented to our group (who are themselves experts in the insurance business) a plan that had identical benefits at a much lower rate. This plan was underwritten by a company called Real Life Insurance Company. The vote went twelve to zero in favor of keeping the Blue Cross coverage. Even though these men knew better, their comments were, "How do we know they'll pay claims—I never heard of Real Life." "Are their reserves large enough to survive a bad year?" "What kind of service can we expect from them?" "You know, Blue Cross people are really delightful to deal with." "Blue Cross may be more expensive, but you can always count on them." Although everybody still complains about the high premiums we pay, nobody is willing to pay a lesser premium to be insured by Real Life Insurance Company.

Ask yourself if you've ever responded to certain situations with thoughts similar to the following: "Will the Sparkler pen last as long as a Sheaffer? Even though it's only half the price, should I buy it?" "Is the Gant shirt really worth the extra cost over the Quaker shirt? Sure it is; it won't shrink, but the Quaker will." "The IBM typewriter costs almost three times as much as the Jones-Corona, but it will probably last ten times as long."

And don't Tretorn tennis shoes feel more comfortable than Ted Ferries? Doesn't Miller's beer have a much smoother taste than Boor's? And, of course, doesn't the Dunhill pipe burn sweeter than the DBD pipe?

We are so presold on the name-brand product that we *know* it's of a much finer quality than the unknown one, and we won't allow ourselves to be convinced otherwise. We don't want to take a chance on the unknown because we fear making a mistake. Since we know that many have benefited from the company's product or service for so many years, we want to continue using it on the grounds that *the majority can't be wrong.* And if they were wrong, we wouldn't feel so bad about making a mistake that everybody else made, too. We just don't want to feel stupid by being the only ones who goofed.

The brand-name image affects everybody. A young student who graduates from the law school at Yale or Harvard in the lower quarter of his class will have a much better chance of getting a job offer from a major law firm than the honors student who made his way through Peabody College by working the night shift at the local fish market. Why? Because the law schools have a proven track record, and it's impressive to introduce the "Yalie" to the firm's clients. After all, nobody asks what your point average was after you've been out of school for ten years, but they *do* ask what university you graduated from!

While on the subject of attorneys, I want to point out how a large, prestigious law firm can often charge its clients a higher rate simply because of its reputation. When the young first-year lawyer from Day, Knight, Black, White, Young and Olds works on your file, you are certainly inclined to feel more comfortable than you would if you were using Joe Blow's one-man law firm, which has been operating for thirty years.

Again, we have another fine example of brand-name image. Even the names of individuals can be brand names.

As a businessman who travels extensively, I must admit I sometimes pay through the nose at restaurants that have brand-name images. In nightclubs I have often begun to enjoy the entertainment only after somebody told me that the singer is a famous star who has appeared on the "Tonight" show with Johnny Carson and at the Grand Hotel in Las Vegas. In fact, on many occasions I thought I was watching third-rate entertainment until I was tipped off that the performer is world-renowned. Certainly, there are thousands of entertainers who get paid only a fraction of what the big-time stars demand, simply because they haven't reached, and perhaps never will reach, the "brand-name image" status. But that's show biz.

Why, you may ask, do I dwell so much on brand-name images? Don't they apply only to national companies and big-time personalities? While they certainly do on a national level, you can do wonders in establishing your own "brand names" with your own product or service.

Virtually all professional people develop reputations for certain specialties. A leading law firm may specialize in corporate law, while another may concentrate on divorce cases. Doctors specialize, and certain accounting firms may develop a local reputation for being strong in tax work, while others may become well known for their corporate-planning abilities. One smart restaurateur will strive to build his reputation on a special dish, such as roast beef; another may attract a certain clientele with his unique salads, or perhaps his internationally famous Kickapoo Cocktail draws the most attention. In the same way, local insurance agents may become specialists in various lines ranging from casualty insurance to pension plans. Real estate brokers can also have different specialties ranging from lower-priced homes to huge industrial parks and shopping center complexes.

All of the above are brand-name images that local business and professional people develop. You don't have to be a multi-billion-dollar corporation to have your own brand-name image. In fact, sometimes a local businessman develops such a strong reputation that national brand names are of little or no value: *his* reputation overrides even that of the giants in the industry. A good example is the local insurance agency that establishes such a fine reputation that its clients don't even know the names of the insurance companies whose policies they buy. "Hell, I can't tell you the name of my automobile policy's company or who I have my life insurance policy with," says a satisfied client. "I have all my insurance with Bill Loman, and I know that whatever he sells me is the best." How many times have you heard similar remarks?"

A really fine clothing store will purposely use only its own private labels instead of national brand names. Again, the local brand-name image overrides that of the giant clothing manufacturers. "I buy all my clothes from Harold Winston," boasts a well-dressed young executive. "If a suit comes from Winston's, I know it's the finest-quality suit that money can buy. You know, I can always spot a suit from Harold Winston's because it has a certain look." Actually, several leading men's stores in the same town may carry the same suit, but under a different label.

I know women who drive from Columbus to Cincinnati, over a four-hour round trip, just to shop at a certain ladies' boutique. They often discover later that other women are wearing identical dresses, acquired from a local dress store in Columbus and bearing a

"No, thank you. I don't drink off-brand whiskey."

different label. In case you're wondering which dresses are less expensive, you guessed it—those purchased in Columbus. Yet, because the Columbus store doesn't have the same winning image as the shop in Cincinnati, it fails to attract clientele.

You've undoubtedly often heard someone remark that you can always spot a home built by such-and-such an architect, decorated by a particular interior decorator, or landscaped by a contractor whose "unique style" is easily recognized and usually associated with the finer homes in a given neighborhood. Some businesses that cater to the carriage trade soon become synonymous with quality, and employing their services becomes a status symbol. These are brand-name images on a local basis, and they are definitely winning images.

Conclusion

In your business or profession it is very important to strive for a brand-name image, but you must single out a certain service or product that you wish to establish as your "specialty." Remember, unless you're General Motors or Federated Department Stores, you can't have something for everybody. Picking out a certain item or two and strongly emphasizing it will encourage people to believe that you've got the best in town. If you really work at it, and constantly tell everybody that you're the best, it won't be long before you will be. Then you'll have your own brand-name image!

Intimidating Images

Certainly images can and *do* intimidate. You should always be fully aware of the images that do, from time to time, intimidate you. And you may want to use images to intimidate others.

Perhaps one of the best examples of intimidating images we all sooner or later experience is the treatment we receive at a fancy French restaurant. No matter what your station in life, unless you're fully prepared to deal with the master French-waiter intimidator, you might as well accept the fact that you will spend a great deal of money and, at the same time, be completely cowed. For the vast majority of us, ordering a complete meal from a French menu is a very uncomfortable and unforgettable experience. Perhaps the waiter's faintly audible French accent or the restaurant's elegant atmosphere makes us feel somewhat awkward, but whatever the reason, most people can be assured of an intimidating experience if they choose to dine at this type of restaurant.

While in New York on a recent business trip, I dined at the ultra-deluxe and expensive Twenty-two Club with W. Clement Roche, my business associate, whose net worth ran into nine figures. He was not accustomed to dining at such a ridiculously expensive restaurant either, since he was a man who was too involved in his business to have developed the finesse required to cope with such nonsense. Being able to order a complete meal in perfect sequence without mispronouncing a word takes a certain amount of exposure and experience. Unfortunately, my wealthy friend made a major mistake when he ordered a round of Cold Duck. The waiter simply shrugged his shoulders and claimed, in an elegant mixture of French and English (he probably grew up in the Bronx), that he never heard of Cold Duck. He then called over another waiter and, after a five-minute conference, they announced, "Gentlemen, although we do not have Cold Duck, we can give you something quite similar."

By this time, people from surrounding tables were snickering at us because we had the audacity to order Cold Duck at the Twenty-two Club. While we weren't sophisticated enough to select a fine wine, we certainly weren't stupid, so we realized we were being laughed at. Clement meekly replied, "Yes, anything similar will be just fine." The waiter returned with a comparable half-bottle that cost approximately ten times the normal cost of Cold Duck. And the two of us didn't say a word!

Throughout my meal, I remained absolutely astonished at what had happened. I had witnessed a very wealthy and powerful man being completely intimidated by a waiter whose weekly income was less than Roche's average hourly earnings! In no other imagi-

"I admit that the food isn't on a par with the Twenty-two Club; but on the other hand, the waiter doesn't intimidate you here."

nable circumstances could Roche be so put down by such a man. I learned a valuable lesson then that I'll always remember: "Be cautious when you're on the other man's home court or you'll get hit right between the eyes."

Believe it or not, I let the same thing happen to me in a similar situation at a deluxe New York jewelry store, Van Clott's, a few months later. I wanted to buy my wife a fine diamond ring because I had not been able to afford to give her one at the time of our engagement. My big mistake was the manner in which I docilely wandered from counter to counter and stared at the beautiful pieces of jewelry without having the courage to ask a clerk for any prices. As I stood bent over a glass case, trying inconspicuously to read a price tag that was not only upside down, but scribbled in code as well, a voice suddenly demanded, "And what can I do for you today?"

As I jumped back and attempted to regain the composure I had lost because of the sudden shock of hearing his voice, I meekly inquired, "H-how much is that ring, sir?" Rarely, if ever, have I called a sales clerk "sir"—particularly a clerk who looks like one of those butlers who always answered the front door of a large mansion in the forties' movies.

"Why, it's merely eighteen thousand dollars. Let me take it out and show it to you."

To this day, I can't believe I actually responded with a sincere, "Is t-that all?"

There have been other occasions when I've suffered the humiliation of being intimidated, and no matter who you are, I am quite sure that you, too, have been in similar situations. Most often, you are trying to act as if you know what you're doing in a particular situation, when, in fact, you actually know very little or nothing. Some of the most frustrating, common, intimidating situations arise when shopping for furniture, buying antiques, or attempting to deal with an interior decorator. It's simply uncanny how some of those male interior decorators can intimidate even the most powerful businessman. This is particularly true when the decorator joins forces with the man's wife, who obviously knows more about furniture than her husband. Of course, she's interested in convincing her husband that he shouldn't be so tight with the buck, which automatically means that he has a two-on-one battle on his hands right from the start.

In order to avoid these awkward moments (which are an inevitable part of life), you should remember some very basic rules. First, keep your sense of humor. Remember that these things aren't really important enough to get upset over, so learn to keep them in proper perspective. Second, let the other party know you're no slouch. Immediately tell him that you're very busy and don't have much time to spend on such trivia (calling his business *trivia* will instantly take away some of the impact of his intimidation—in fact, you can make him the "intimidatee" at this point, if you so desire). Then announce that you are the chairman of the board of the Mystic Corporation (vice president, director, or whatever your title may be), but do it in such a manner that he knows *you are important*. What you are actually striving for is to be in the driver's seat —that way you can control him from the very beginning. A word of caution, however: don't try to bluff and pretend you know a great deal about his field if, in fact, you really don't. Once you're discovered, as you surely will be, he'll dominate you, and it will be all uphill from then on. Third, and perhaps the best advice: avoid all such situations whenever possible so that you are never made to feel awkward. Let your wife deal with the furniture people, the interior decorators, and the French waiters. And if you're single, instead of trying to impress your date, let her select the dinner from the French menu. If she can't do it, then she certainly can't think any less of you because you can't either!

By now you should be in the mood to understand exactly how to use an intimidating image and make it work *for you*. (And, if you happen to be an interior decorator, a French waiter, or a furniture salesman in a high-priced furniture store, I believe you'll still have much to learn if you continue to read further!)

As I stated earlier, "Be cautious when you're on the other man's home court or you'll get hit right between the eyes." What does that tell you about the times when you'll be on your own home court? Most of the time, this is where you'll be operating. For this reason, you should learn to take advantage of this position. *You* are the expert when the other fellow treads on your territory, not him. If your profession happens to be law, remember that this person is coming to your office to seek your advice. He is willing to pay you because you know more about law than he does. If he didn't think this was so, he obviously wouldn't have come to you in the first place. Regardless of what you do, whether you're an accountant, a doctor, a building contractor, a florist, a funeral director, a pharmacist, or a used car salesman, you must remember that *you know more about your field than the individual who comes to do business with you*. (If you don't, then none of this matters because you'll eventually lose either your business or your job.) Therefore you should be completely confident and act with assurance. You'll then be in a position where you cannot be intimidated; indeed, if you so desire, you can now intimidate others.

Such tactics may sound a bit unsportsmanlike, and, in certain cases, they very well may be. Yet on certain occasions they're justified because they do get results. If you are very subtle, you won't destroy any goodwill you may have had with your intimidatee.

Many people believe that doctors are the champion intimidators. I thoroughly enjoy watching a doctor giving orders to his patient to do this or that. He might say, for instance, "I don't care how busy you are. I want you to go straight to the hospital *this moment* and we're going to give you a thorough examination and find out what's giving you those headaches. I don't care if it takes all week to find out."

When the doctor speaks with such authority, his patient does exactly what he's told. On the other hand, what would happen if the same doctor said, "Look, Sam, are you really too busy to spend a few days in the hospital? You really need an examination, and I think it would be a good idea for you to go in."

You would probably expect Sam to say, "Doc, I don't give a damn what you think. I've got a big business to run. I'll get back with you in a couple of months during my slow season, and if I still have headaches, I'll do as you say." Not only do patients obey the doctor who intimidates, but they love him for it as well. Why? Because he gets results.

If doctors aren't the best intimidators, then attorneys must be. Of course, since they know the laws, the contracts, and the precedents, they are in the driver's seat all the way. You go to an attorney only when you have a problem, so from the very beginning he—at least if he's good—controls the situation. The same thing holds true when you take your tax problem to a good CPA firm. When the SEC or IRS bears down on you, if you don't do exactly as you're instructed, they're going to intimidate you whether you like it or not!

The consultant will behave in basically the same way. After all, he's the expert and you're the one with the problem. When we started our insurance company, American Executive Life, we were completely at the mercy of an actuarial consulting firm, and believe me, they played the role of intimidator to the hilt! As I look back, we were in over our heads because we were completely relying on what they told us, and we had absolutely no knowledge of whether or not they were calling the right shots. The more business we did with them, the deeper in we went. Our survival in business actually depended on their consultation, and their advice was so complex and completely foreign to us that there was no way we could ever really fully understand what they were telling us. We had to have complete faith that they knew what they were doing, and let me tell you, that's a bad position to be in. Never again do I want to find myself there.

Other consultants will intimidate their clients with their specialized knowledge, their Ph.D.'s, their track record, or any other tools they may have that create an intimidating image. I sincerely believe that they must use these images to keep their clients in line because, once a person begins to use the services of a consultant, he rarely or never runs his business again without him!

Good salesmen also realize the value of intimidation. Any top life insurance agent who's worth his salt will intimidate his clients. Remember, he's selling a product that nobody enjoys buying, and the prospect's first reaction after hearing the sales presentation is to delay making a decision. Every experienced salesman knows that his prospect will most likely "cool off" if the sale isn't closed while there's still a spark of fire. In most cases, intimidation is the most effective way to close the sale. "Mr. Milquetoast," says Harold Hill, the leading producer for Anvil Life for the past sixteen years, "you surely can't be serious about wanting to discuss with your wife how much life insurance you need. I was under the impression that you were a decisive man. After all, you run a big business, and you certainly don't call your wife every time you need to order more inventory, do you? I know you wear the pants in your family. That's what I like so much about dealing with businessmen. Why, the little guy can never make a move without talking it over with his old lady. But I know you're not that type."

"Harold," says Mr. Milquetoast, "let's raise that amount from six hundred to seven hundred and fifty thousand. And do you need my check for the annual payment now or can I just give you half and the balance when I'm accepted?"

As you can see, intimidation *does* initiate success.

I know many outstanding salesmen who sell by intimidating their customers in a very subtle way. Some of them aren't even very subtle about it, but they are all good, and the same people continue to buy from them. Evidently, few people object too strongly to being intimidated by such salesmen.

Other salesmen often come right out and tell their customers that they're the best producer in the area and know more about their product than anyone else. People take pride in telling their friends that they do business with the number-one Chevy salesman in town, or the top mutual fund salesman or stockbroker, so don't be afraid to tell your customers how good you are. If you listen to what people have to say, you'll discover that they like to brag about how good the salesman was who sold them their new home, their new car, or their new television. If you want to be sure they know just how good you are, *tell them*. Make it part of your sales presentation—build up your own image. If you don't, who will?

Obviously, there are many other ways used every

day in business to intimidate people. One of the most common intimidating images is that of the banker, which is blatantly apparent during a loan discussion. Of course, here again is a situation in which you are going to the other party to get something you must have. You undergo a similar experience when you go to a dentist to get a tooth pulled because you're writhing in pain. If you're out on the freeway with motor trouble and must be towed into the only service station in the area, you're at the mercy of the dealer. In each of these examples, and in countless others like them, the victim is placed in a position where he will undoubtedly build up an intimidating image in his own mind *even prior to meeting his intimidator*.

Other well-planned techniques of intimidating have been discussed so often in other books that they'll just be touched upon lightly here. We've all heard of the so-called tycoon who arranges his office furniture in such a way that his intimidatee has to sit in a lower seat and awkwardly look up at his intimidator. Or his desk is in front of a window, forcing his intimidatee to look into the sunshine or glaring light. There's also the type who raises his voice and uses vulgar language to bully others, as well as the one who insults practically everybody with whom he deals. In my opinion, these methods of intimidation are really cover-ups for what are obviously the intimidator's deep-seated emotional problems.

There's also the executive-type intimidator who never visits another man's office without being accompanied by at least one assistant. Jack Leggstrong, the chairman of W. T. Lee Department Stores, is a good example of this type. For any meeting Leggstrong always had with him several members of the company, usually a vice president, some accountants, and at least one attorney. Once, while in New York, a good friend of mine approached Leggstrong about a possible merger. Since the deal couldn't go through at a formal meeting, my friend suggested that they meet for an informal breakfast in order to work things out. Leggstrong agreed to come to my friend's hotel suite, but to my friend's surprise, five other men showed up with him! Is this an example of good intimidation, or does Leggstrong strike you as a man who lacks the necessary confidence to act on his own?

Fred Bellman, an all-time great life insurance salesman, normally takes his own accountant to a prospect's office. In most cases, his clients are impressed by the fact that he can afford the luxury of having his own accountant, and Fred's professional image is therefore strengthened. Quite frankly, I think he really takes the accountant along to intimidate his prospects. He reminds me of the tennis player who wears an expensive warm-up suit to the match and carries three tennis racquets. These don't make him a better tennis player, but he does succeed in intimidating his opponent.

Conclusion

I hope I've given you some good tips on how to recognize situations in which you leave yourself open to intimidation. Also, if it's your style, you may have learned some new techniques for intimidating others. Be warned, however, that you won't win any popularity contests with your new intimidating image. Yet, like everything else, you must decide what's best for your long-range goals, and what will help you achieve the most effective results. Remember, winners aren't always nice guys!

11   A Winning Self-Image

If you want a winning image with others, your first concern must be a winning *self*-image. The individual who has a losing self-image will never be able to project a winning image to others. He may be able to fool some people for a while, but his poor self-image will eventually make it impossible for him to relate favorably to others. Throughout the ages, great philosophers have stated, "You are what you think you are." How true this is when you apply it to your own winning self-image. It is imperative for you to have a good image of yourself if you want to create the same impression in others.

No matter who you are, everything worthwhile will depend on your own self-image. Your happiness will be based on it. You will live only one life, and in order to enjoy and value it, you must have a winning self-image. Since we can all actually choose how we want to think of ourselves, we should try to have positive, winning thoughts. Because a good self-image is the basis of both success and happiness, this chapter is the most fundamental in *Winning Images*. In your own attempt to build a winning image you must begin with the self—otherwise, the image you strive for will be supported by nothing but a sand foundation.

Any athlete will tell you that you must *know* you're a winner in order to *be* one. To many, this kind of message will sound like double-talk, but it contains an essential truth. Although you can apply this same message to anything in life, I will use athletics as the basis for illustrating my thoughts about self-images because sports involve physical exertion that is ultimately transformed into definite, conclusive results.

Boxing is an excellent example. The results of a boxing match can easily be measured: one man wins and the other man loses. Is it always, however, the man with the most strength, speed, and endurance who wins the fight? I think not, for I believe it is possible for the less physical man to be the winner if he has a better self-image. The man who knows he's going to win will have a marked advantage over the man who doesn't possess the same confidence. In boxing jargon this is called "being psyched up," but I refer to it as having a winning self-image. The timing of the boxer with a losing self-image will be off: he'll pull his punches, and he'll shy away from his opponent because he fears him. A winning self-image gives its possessor extra stamina and sharpens his reflexes. It make the adrenaline flow to give him that something extra so that he finds himself doing everything right. When your body and mind work together perfectly, *you can't lose!*

In golf, all the pros will tell you that the game is 99 percent in the mind. Golfers who weigh less than 130 pounds have demonstrated that they can drive the ball as far as the 200-pounders. The physical capacity of a golfer isn't really the decisive factor. Again, the difference is determined by a winning self-image. *Knowing* that you're going to play a good round of golf makes all the difference. If you don't believe in yourself, you'll squirm and soon discover that your footing isn't correct. Then you'll move your hands around and change your grip. Soon you'll lose your concentration. It doesn't take long for even the professional golfer to go into a serious slump under such conditions. It always amazes me how even a pro can shoot a subpar round and the very next day have a difficult time breaking 80.

You can apply this same principle to tennis. What is it that causes a tennis pro to lose 6–0 and then immediately win a love set over his opponent? It can't be a physical phenomenon because a drastic change in both players from one set to the other within the space of an hour is impossible.

To win in sports, *you must believe that you are a winner*. If you're going to win the Indianapolis 500, you must first *know* you're going to win it. In order to high-jump seven feet six inches, you must *know* you can do it. And until the mile-runners broke the four-minute mile, they had to *know* it could be done and that they could do it.

The winning self-image concept can be applied to any endeavor. You're never going to be a 4.0 student, no matter how hard you try, unless you can look at yourself in the mirror and say, "I am a 4.0 student!" And you won't sell $5 million worth of life insurance until you convince yourself that you're a $5-million producer. You'll never pass a bar examination, you'll never become a CPA, and you'll never achieve any other major goal until you believe that you are capable of doing it. In fact, I would never be able to finish writing this book if I didn't believe that I was fully capable of doing so.

When my father and I wrote our first book, *How to Be the Complete Professional Salesman,* most of my supposedly good friends criticized me and said, "What's a salesman like you writing a book for? That's silly!" Some books are probably never finished because of similar comments about the writer's ability to complete the manuscript. In fact, I would venture to say that the vast majority of manuscripts are never completed because of the author's poor self-image. Lack of confidence is a more serious impediment to finishing a book than lack of talent. In our case, however, we were absolutely sure from the very beginning that we could write a book and get it published. We never had the slightest doubt. While there are critics who don't believe in my writing talents, there are no disbelievers in my winning self-image, and if I had to make a choice between one or the other, I'd take the winning self-image over talent any day of the week. Obviously, for success, the two must go hand in hand, but with the right self-image, you'll soon develop the necessary skill to do *any* job.

What comes first—the chicken or the egg? People come to me and say over and over: "When I have the success I'm after, I'll have the winning image!" Unfortunately, that's not the way life works. You must develop the winning self-image before you can ever achieve the success you desire. Furthermore, there are definite ways by which you can develop a winning self-image. To begin, you must rid yourself of all fears and self-doubts. Fears are easy to throw away once you put them in their proper perspective. If you analyze them, you'll often find that they're really silly and immaterial, and the vast majority don't even exist except in your mind. The fear of failure is perhaps the most common, but if you refuse to accept failure, you will never fail. Once such self-doubts are completely removed from your mind, you can concentrate on something much more important: getting the results you're after.

Secondly, in order to develop the confidence necessary for a winning self-image, you must fully prepare yourself so that you are 100 percent convinced that you are the best. If you are fully prepared for any situation, you will possess a winning self-image because you're truly ready to cope with any obstacles that may arise. *Knowing* how well prepared you are is what makes such an image possible. *Being fully prepared grants you the right to have a winning image.* You'll commit a serious error if you aren't completely prepared because *you can't fool yourself.*

What a difference it makes when you walk into a man's office with confidence! The salesman who hasn't done his homework properly has good reason to be full of doubts and trepidation. But the man who knows he can handle any curve thrown at him has everything going for him. Not only will he know it, but everybody around him will sense his confidence, and they, too, will react favorably. "Charisma," "positive thinking," and "enthusiasm" have often been used to characterize this confidence, and they all mean the same thing: *a winning self-image.* And it's contagious. The salesman who has it will give his customer the confidence to make a firm decision. The salesman who lacks it will find himself with a prospect who is unable to make up his mind. The salesman's own self-image will actually be mimicked by his customer.

The next time you watch a star performer on stage or TV, look for this inner quality. I don't care whom you pick—all great show business personalities have it. It is their winning self-image that allows them to rise above the thousands of others in their field who never get their careers off the launching pad. The ones who never quite make it will tell you they never got the right break, they weren't at the right place at the right time. It's no wonder they cop such a plea; they recognize that the big stars aren't any more talented than they are, and they can't seem to identify this intangible winning quality—*self-image*.

I know a middle-aged divorcée, Doris Knight, who's on the plump side and not very good-looking. But Doris doesn't think she's overweight and unattractive. In fact, she considers herself quite sexy and appealing to every man she meets. Because she thinks this way, she really does have a certain "look" and her body movements do something to any male who watches her. Is it the way Doris walks, or the way she sits? I don't really know, but there's something about her that is radiant and definitely attracts men. Certainly, her facial expressions and her soft voice have nothing whatsoever to do with how Doris would be in bed; nevertheless, because she thinks she's sexy, *she is sexy*. Doris has a winning self-image.

Another girl I know, Jill St. Paul, has perfect measurements and an exquisite face. But she doesn't know it, and she always walks around with a deadpan expression. Jill has poor posture, and even walks in a peculiar, unbecoming manner. She can't even look you straight in the eye. Jill thinks she's getting old, although she's only thirty-two. She acts much older than her years. It's absolutely astonishing to see how a poor self-image can change the appearance of a girl, who, if she had a winning self-image, would be considered a knockout.

A winning self-image not only makes a big difference in your physical appearance, but it also plays a major role in how old you look and feel. There is a great deal of truth in the expression, "You're only as young as you feel." Feeling old is, for the most part, only a state of mind. I have seen people who are young at the age of seventy-five and others who are old at forty-five. Besides, age is so relative—I can remember hearing a sports announcer saying, "The aging, over-worked old man walks slowly away from the mound in defeat." The pitcher he was referring to was a man who was thirty-seven years old! About seven years later, after he had retired from baseball, this same pitcher ran for the U.S. Congress. The media described him as being "young," "refreshing," and "eager."

A winning self-image will make a big difference in everything about you—your appearance, how you feel, and how you perform. All of these are involved in making you a winner when you relate to others. Take, for example, Glenn Johns, an up-and-coming young businessman who had just begun his own plumbing-supply business and needed a large loan from his banker. Glenn radiated self-confidence, and he fully believed he was going to be a huge success in business. Don't you think this self-image would help persuade his banker to loan him money, even if making the loan risked a fifty-fifty chance? "Glenn, I've looked over your financial figures," his banker told him, "and, as you well know, our main concern is your ability to make these loan repayments according to this schedule. Are you sure that your cash flow will be able to handle it?"

Glenn smiled and quietly replied, "Believe me, I feel that I have actually been quite conservative in my profit projections. Let me state that I have a very fine business right now, and I certainly wouldn't want to expand and get myself heavily into debt if I didn't have complete faith in our profit picture. Without question, we've just begun to scratch the surface of what this business is capable of doing."

The banker looked over the projections and stated, "Glenn, I believe in you. We're going to go out on the limb because this bank thinks you have a great future."

If Glenn Johns had hemmed and hawed and told the banker, "Well, I dunno, who knows what's a sure thing these days? I work hard, and I'll do my best to make this business succeed, but I can't give you any guarantees that it's gonna work out," his poor self-image would have had an adverse effect on his chances of convincing the banker to go along with him on this borderline case.

A winning self-image makes a big difference in everything you do. It will always get you favorable results whether you're applying for a new job, being considered for a big promotion, or walking into an office to tell the receptionist you're there to see her boss. People will see you as you see yourself. If you believe that you are important, others will treat you as a VIP.

I can remember spending two days in the field with a salesman in Arizona who claimed that the people in Phoenix were not receptive to salesmen. During the first few hours when we made "cold calls" on businessmen, I let him make the approach and he was right— the reception was terrible. Then I made the approach, and we got in to talk with every businessman we called on, or, if they were busy at that time, we were able to set up a firm appointment for the next day. The salesman said to me, "Bob, I don't understand it. I guess you're just lucky and called on friendly, receptive people. I had all the bad calls." Actually, luck had nothing to do with my success. I had a winning self-image and he didn't. Even though we both approached prospects with an identical presentation, I projected a winning self-image and he projected a losing one.

"Homer," I said to him, "when I approached the

receptionist and told her that I wanted to speak with her employer because I had highly confidential information to discuss with him, she told him, 'There's a Mr. Shook here to see you. It's very important; you'd better talk with him now.' When you said the same words, she informed her employer, 'There's a salesman out here wanting to see you. Should I tell him you're busy and not to call back?" Homer continued to insist that I had called on the easy prospects. He couldn't understand why I was so "lucky" when he had been having such a bad streak for six months prior to my arrival in Phoenix to work with him!

Our agency conducted an experiment concerning a similar matter. We had several agents read exactly the same script over the telephone for the purpose of setting up appointments with prospects, and the results of their calls fluctuated vastly. It wasn't the sound of the man's voice that made the difference (one salesman who had the voice of a radio announcer got poor results), but the confidence he transmitted to the prospect at the other end of the line. Yes, a winning self-image can be projected even by phone!

A winning self-image has a major impact on everything from selling to doing open-heart surgery. Dr. Denton Cooley clearly expressed his thoughts on the subject when I asked him whom he considered to be the world's best heart surgeons.* "When I'm asked to name the world's three best heart surgeons," he responded, "I have trouble deciding who the other two are. Of course," he added quickly, "I'm only joking when I say this. But, in a sense, I guess I really do have a kind of supreme confidence. And frankly, in my business I think you *have* to have it. Self-confidence is absolutely necessary for a heart surgeon

* Total Commitment, p. 232.

because he has to be decisive. He has to make decisions quickly and then be ready to act on them. In open-heart surgery," he explained, "there is so little time available to get the job done. Even the mechanical devices we use to support life while we're operating can give us only a limited amount of time. So, the slightest hesitation . . . the failure to make a quick decision . . . a quivering hand . . . any of these can cause irrevocable damage. In other words, a lack of confidence can be *fatal*."

Conclusion

To many readers, a winning self-image may seem egotistical. If you feel this way, remember that having a strong ego isn't necessarily an undesirable quality. There's a significant difference between having a winning self-image and being an egomaniac. Thinking highly of yourself is a desirable trait. Unless you feel good about yourself, you have no right to expect others to see good in you. All great achievers believe in themselves. If they didn't, they would lead lives of mediocrity. Study yourself. By taking a complete inventory of your strengths as well as your weaknesses, you will be in a realistic position to make the changes necessary for becoming the person you want to be and for creating the winning image you want for your business. I strongly believe that every person has more good qualities than bad. You must discover your own positive traits, and your sincere belief in them will help you in building a winning image. Always remember: *Knowing that you're a winner is essential in winning.*

"Dear Diary: My self-image is down. Nobody addressed me as 'Your Majesty' all day."

12 Your Spouse—an Asset or a Liability

When you took your spouse for better or for worse, you very probably were not thinking in terms of his or her image. But you should never underestimate the influence your mate will have on your own image. Though I am not suggesting that you head straight for the divorce court if on completing this chapter you discover that your spouse is a liability, I do believe that you should be fully aware of the impact your husband or wife can have on your image. You may even discover that he or she is one of your strongest assets, but one that you haven't been using properly to enhance your image. This chapter will be divided into two parts—one dealing with the wife; the other, with the husband.

A. Your Wife

Let's get it straight from the very beginning—we're talking about your image, not about your acual ability to perform effectively on the job. Obviously, your wife's capacity to influence your image will not determine your ability to perform as an attorney, an executive, or a CPA, but she will make a major difference as far as your image is concerned, and this, in turn, will directly affect the long-range success of your career. Your wife plays a major role in many business/social functions that are crucial to your career. The way she impresses others will absolutely affect their opinion of you. To repeat, this will be for better or for worse—only rarely will her influence be neutral.

If you are a professional man, the business-related social events you attend with your wife are important not only because of the presence of your clients, but because new prospects will be present as well. The impressions that those would-be clients and their wives get of you and your wife may determine how successful you are in convincing them to use your services. If they find your wife utterly charming, they will react favorably; if she completely turns them off, your chances of doing business with them will be greatly diminished.

Obviously, if your wife is loud and obnoxious, there may be very little you can do to convert her into a plus factor. A complete revamping of her personality may be an impossible job. Likewise, if she's completely out of it, there may be no hope of ever raising her intelligence to a level where she can communicate effectively with your clients. Naturally, these are extreme cases because it can safely be assumed that, along with your ability to rise to the executive level, you also had the intelligence to marry a woman who was your intellectual equal. If not, then I suggest that you either lock your wife in a closet or leave her home whenever possible. I might also suggest that both of you avoid business-connected social functions whenever possible. It's always better to have people wonder why you didn't come rather than for you to wish you hadn't.

In most cases, however, there is a good deal you can do to improve your wife's poor image. If, for example, you don't approve of her behavior after one too many drinks, then you must be careful not to allow her to overindulge. If she doesn't say the right things because she's not well informed about business matters, then it's your responsibility to educate her properly. Assuming she's of average intelligence, she'll pick things up quickly, and you'll be amazed at her capability to discuss any subject regarding business as long as it is not too technical. And highly technical subjects aren't really supposed to be discussed at such affairs.

It's often wise to advise your wife not to talk about controversial subjects at business/social functions. Depending on the crowd, religion and politics can get her into considerable trouble. If she's a die-hard women's libber, she can not only make your male clients feel like fools, but she can make you look like one as well. All too often I see wives at business/social gatherings who seem to be looking for any opportunity to put down their husbands in front of others. Such put-downs are damaging to your career, which surely is not the intention of your loving wife. I suggest that a long talk with her is in order so that she may fully realize that both you and she will lose in the long run if she doesn't change her attitude. Obviously, this kind of problem stems from the absence of mutual communication, and if you don't communicate with your wife, I can see no reason why you should expect her to communicate with your business associates and would-be clients.

Naturally, your wife should act like a lady at all times. A good rule of thumb is: "As long as she's a lady, you'll have an asset, not a liability." Of course, her appearance will have a great deal to do with the impression she makes on others. Without question, the way she dresses is just as important as the way you do. Because women seem so much more clothes-conscious than men, buying a beautiful wardrobe for your wife, if you can afford it, is an excellent investment. Having her dressed in very fine clothes and smartly bedecked with appropriate jewelry will create a winning image and *make you look successful.* Your client's wife will usually have a strong influence on her husband, and she will comment to him about whether or not your wife was acceptably dressed. "Did you notice the exquisite dress Tony Fields' wife was wearing, dear?" she'll ask her husband upon leaving the party. "Did you know that Cornelia was wearing a Halston dress? She's such a stunning dresser. Why, Corn is just a real smart, all-around girl!"

On the other hand, if your wife dresses like a tramp or has no taste, she will get a negative reaction from your client's wife. "Did you see Jack Hill's wife, Jill? Where in the world did he ever pick her up? He seemed so refined, but she looked like a hooker!"

It's never appropriate for your wife to try to be the sexiest woman in town. Quite often, understated but up-to-date attire will make a more favorable impression on even the men. Sure, having your wife dress in a gown that "lets it all hang out" may create a sensation and cause many of your would-be clients to want to go to bed with her, but it won't motivate them to call your office in the morning because they want to do business with you!

Many wives are their husband's biggest asset in attracting new clients because of their active role in the community. Since they serve on several boards, they make strong contacts with many of the community's most prominent citizens. These highly capable women develop friendships with the wives of very successful business leaders, who, in turn, are introduced to you. I know several women who are responsible for bringing many top clients to their husbands' practices. In fact, they have attracted top clients whom their husbands would *never* have met without this kind of contact. It's always good for your image whenever your wife gets her name and picture on the society page of the newspaper for her civic and charitable activities.

Your wife's ability to entertain properly also helps to give you a winning image. Her charming personality at a dinner party will greatly impress everyone, particularly if she prepares and serves a beautiful meal. Those little personal touches she adds to her preparation of the dinner normally get the most favorable "ooh's and ah's." Another great winning image can be the manner in which she has decorated your home. People usually associate tasteful decor with good breeding, so it's important that your wife and her decorator collaborate to give your home a quality look. All of us have been in homes that impress us and suggest that the host and hostess are refined people. Other homes in which the same amount of money has been spent for furnishings and decoration give us the impression that we are in houses of ill-repute!

How many times after leaving someone's home has your wife, like a broken record, said, "Boy, did you notice the beautiful area rug they had in their entrance? And wasn't that needlepoint on the sofa lovely? I bet that silverware must have cost a small fortune for each setting. And they must have a huge investment tied up in their paintings. They're all original." Knowing that your wife reacts like this should make you realize that other wives probably go through the same routine. As you can see, your wife's good homemaking and her talent for entertaining guests in your home are definite factors in creating a winning image.

B. Your Husband

In determining whether your husband is an asset or a liability for your image, you can apply much the same criteria I suggested a husband use in evaluating his wife. You, too, must decide whether to go it without him and keep your husband locked up in the closet, or whether he can be a contributing factor in building your winning image. Obviously, you can apply the same rules as previously mentioned in judging his ability to converse intelligently with your business associates. In many cases, a professional woman who marries a man with less intelligence must suffer because of his knack for saying the wrong things whenever he's with her clients. If he's sexist, he may even resent her success, and purposely downgrade her in the presence of important business contacts. Other husbands will belittle their wives' professions and talk about their own careers, even though they completely bore their listeners.

Bertha Byrd, an up-and-coming middle-aged executive, started as a typist for a large publishing company, and is now a senior editor. Her husband, Jay, is the manager of a local Ford dealership garage. "I tell you," shouts Jay, "you people don't have any idea why the costs of repairing automobiles are so high. You don't know it, but it's your fault." He continues to bore Bertha's important associates at a cocktail party until

"One wrong word out of you and we're going home and you're going straight to the closet!"

she finally manages to change the subject. But in his persistence Jay screams, "If you publishers want a great idea, why don't you have me write a book on the auto repair industry?" Bertha winces again and decides that in the future she will either do a solo act at such functions or not attend them at all.

If you think Bertha has problems, they're mild when compared to those caused by Pattie Berger's husband, Ham. He's constantly telling dirty jokes, spilling his drinks, and pinching all the women. Such a husband must be spoken to, and it's up to the wife to keep him well informed so that he can intelligently discuss her business. Again, communication with him is fundamental to your image. Such husbands, however, may purposely want to destroy their wives' careers. They may feel their manhood is being threatened by their wives' professionalism, and, for this reason, shaping up a spouse may be more difficult for women than for men. If this is your problem, then you must be aware of the damaging effect your husband has on the image you are trying to build.

On the other hand, just as a wife can be an asset to her husband's image, he can also be one to hers. This is particularly true when he enjoys a similar VIP position in his field. Such a dynamic combination can be a winning image-builder for both husband and wife.

Conclusion

Your spouse can be an asset or a liability in your efforts to develop a winning image. The two of you must communicate with each other in order for the other party to be aware of how he or she should communicate with your associates and clients. The most important thing to remember is that your spouse must always be able to relate effectively to them. Having a spouse who has "a nose in the air" can be just as damaging as being married to the dummy who always says the wrong thing. You must learn to work together because you are really a team, aren't you?

13   A Chapter on Sex

I wish I had a nickel for every person who told me that my first two books would have sold much better had they contained a chapter on Sex. From the way they talked, such a chapter would have made both books best sellers. For those readers—and for any other readers who automatically pick up a book and want to read the sexy parts first—this chapter is completely devoted to sex.

It is true that sex plays a major role in our lives. In fact, many theories on the subject claim that everything we do stems from our sex drive. While I don't intend to expand on such theories, I do recognize that sex is a very popular pastime and to include it in a book will definitely be a plus factor in helping sales.

To the disappointment of those who may be looking forward to reading hard-core pornography, this chapter will concentrate on sex and its relationship to your career. I will not, however, cover the subject of sex images since they are already overplayed and do not apply to careers (unless, of course, you're a prostitute, a professional entertainer, a model, or employed in some other field where your sex appeal is paramount in attracting customers to do business with you).

Actually, my views on the subject are rather provincial. I strongly believe in the old Mexican proverb: "Don't dance on the table from which you eat." Perhaps you have heard a slightly different version of this quote since there are many translations, but they all say the same thing: *Don't play around at work.* In short, I don't care what your pleasures are on your off-time, but when you're working, you must concentrate on getting the maximum results in your work, *not in your sex life!*

Although most people today try to create an image that suggests they're far from prudish about sex, don't make the mistake of assuming that people will think more highly of you as a business or professional person because your love affairs have become legendary. Too many men think that they are impressing their co-workers and clients with stories of their many conquests, when, in fact, they are creating a losing image. These same men are on the make for every female they encounter in business, even female clients. Short-range benefits may result from such love affairs, but I can assure you that such extracurricular activities more often than not seriously damage your long-range image. In fact, this kind of hanky-panky is so ill-chosen that I can't think of anything worse, barring an affair with your mother-in-law!

Truman Blue is a sales representative for Straight Arrow Company, a leading manufacturer of ladies' dresses. Tru travels the states of Georgia and Florida, and has at least one girl friend in each city. He averages three nights of out-of-town lodging each week, and, according to the "Tru Blue legend," never sleeps alone at these times. Tru's wife and four children have yet to hear about his now-notorious reputation as a womanizer, but it's only a matter of time, probably, before some lovesick gal calls his wife, Sue. Because of Tru's business exposure to numerous women each day he has compiled a personal black phonebook that I understand is larger than some of the telephone books in the small Georgia towns he visits. In some of the larger department stores in Atlanta and Miami, Tru has been known to have as many as three romances going at the same time. He often carries on these affairs with buyers and assistants from the same store, and loves to brag about his lovemaking in the stockrooms. "Even standing up during the lunch hour!" he boasts.

Romeos like Tru Blue have a habit of broadcasting how well they score, and it doesn't take long for every other traveling salesman in the territory to know all their stories because they're always good material for conversation when salesmen meet in cocktail lounges at the end of the day. Neither does it take long for some female buyer to get that "jilted" feeling when she figures out that she's not the only one Tru's been shacking up with. Most likely, a department head or an executive of a key account won't see any humor in Tru's escapades. Perhaps down in the Bible Belt where Tru operates, an important customer might feel it's morally wrong for him to have extracurricular affairs with all the local Southern belles. Or a jealous sales manager may resent Tru's "fringe benefits." Obviously, many will think Tru is a dishonest person because he's cheating on his wife. The repercussions of Tru's activities will always be far greater than the few minor, short-range benefits he gains from his image as a ladies' man. Sure, he may be getting a larger order from Stacy's Department Store because he's "in good with the cute redheaded buyer on the fourth floor," but isn't it just as likely that she'll cut down the order or cancel the store's account with Straight Arrow when their love affair cools off?

In spite of what often appears to be rampant promiscuity in our present American society, infidelity is still frowned upon by a great number of people. While I don't intend to discuss the moral aspects of such activities, I do believe that the subject of sex is quite relevant in this discussion of images. You must consider the reactions of others and *how you appear from their point of view*. If you are playing around, you must surely realize that there are a significant number of people who, when they become familiar with your promiscuous reputation, will mark you down as an individual of poor character. Just how much this attitude will affect you is anybody's guess, but even if only a handful of important people feel this way toward you, your career can be hindered or ultimately ruined. When you consider its consequences, promiscuity in business can create such a damaging image that your long-range success may be severely diminished. Although your sexual conquests may sound good in the locker room, do you really think you'll win any popularity contests by establishing a reputation as a tomcat? Do you personally have great respect for such an individual? Is this the kind of person you would trust? Many so-called modern-thinking people loathe such conduct, even though they pretend to go along with the swinger mentality.

It's important to realize that, in many circles, sex is in and acting prudishly about it is taboo. Yet only ten years ago the sex scenes and language employed in today's GP movies would have been banned. Similarly, the near-nudity seen on beaches as well as at cocktail parties would have been considered obscene a few years ago, and anyone so exposed would have been subject to arrest. Yet it does not follow that people who seem to go along with the times have all adopted the "new morality." Revolutionary changes in our attitudes toward sex within such a short period of time don't really revise everyone's deep-rooted, ingrained philosophies. A person who seems to admire another man's sexual campaigns may actually think them contemptible and distrust the man for treating sex so casually. Since sex is a subject people tend to joke about, you often cannot know what they really feel or think. What is important is that you realize that you cannot know how another person may judge you if you come on as a playboy. For this reason, why expose yourself to the kind of ill-will that can seriously injure your image? You must always ask yourself how much you have to gain and how much you have to lose.

I, for one, happen to think that advertising the fact that you're a swinger is simply a matter of poor taste. To repeat, such an image, besides suggesting that you're unreliable and unstable, may also cause people to consider you immoral and incapable of being trusted, especially if you're married. Who's going to be impressed with your conquests? Some married men may be jealous of what you're getting away with, and single men will disrespect you because they won't understand why you got married if you wanted to run around.

Jacques Strapp is one of the great quarterbacks in the NFL and he practically built an international reputation for his sexual activities in show business and high-society circles throughout America. He does commercials that clearly promote him as a "stud," and he's even done a few nude scenes in movies. Chris

Cross, on the other hand, is also a great quarterback, but as an ex-Sunday school teacher and father of four, his image is completely the opposite of Strapp's. Cross works hard to stay in shape and follows strict training rules, while Strapp parties it up with a different starlet every night. So far, however, he's still managed to stay on top in the NFL. Both men are well respected as fine athletes, but which one do you think will be respected in later years after the end of his football career? I can't help admiring Cross, for when he was compared with Strapp on a talk show after the season ended he said, "I enjoy sex every bit as much as Jacques, but I just happen to enjoy it with the *same* woman!" That was a great comment, and he obviously scored well with many fans because of it.

I am always amazed at the number of salesmen who tell me fantastic stories about being propositioned by sex-starved females. According to them, this happens every day of the week. I'm particularly astonished at the door-to-door salesmen who claim they were invited into the housewife's bedroom, or had beautiful women, wearing only a towel that always seems to fall down, greet them at the door. I personally made thousands of similar calls when I was in my twenties, and I was never propositioned by a single housewife. Since I consider myself more attractive than many of the salesmen who boasted of such experiences, I can't help but think, if these stories are even partially true, that the salesmen encouraged the propositions by making either a subtle remark or the first move. I firmly believe that had they made their calls for strictly business reasons, the housewives would not have propositioned them. When you're working for a living, you should be concentrating on your business, not on having a good time!

Many doctors have told me about similar proposi-

tions made by their patients and nurses, and attorneys have told me about love-starved divórcées who not only seek their legal advice, but desire other "services" as well. Again, in all likelihood these propositions are either initiated or encouraged by a man who has more than business on his mind at the time.

A woman hoping to further her career must also remember that the only thing to be thinking about when she's on the job is *her work*. She must forget the fact that she's a woman and working with men. When it comes to job performance, she must not think in terms of the difference in the sexes. Only when she develops this frame of mind will she be most effective in her capacity as a working woman.

Certainly, we've all heard about the young starlet's rise to stardom because she slept with the right director. Perhaps some girls have actually gotten their big break this way, but it's highly unlikely that they stayed on top very long if the public didn't accept them on the basis of their performances as actresses. Many women still believe that "you have to sleep with the right men" if you hope to get ahead in this world. Of course, many women who never achieve the success they seek use this common excuse to cop a plea, just as many men complain all their lives that they never got a break or that "you have to be at the right place at the right time" in order to be successful. Both have to realize that getting ahead in this world takes brains and commitment, not "natural talents."

If you are a female reader who is going to rely on my theories in your efforts to reach the top of your field, I urge you to adhere to a "plain Jane" dress code. You must always remember that your work is your number-one concern, and unless you want men to look upon you as a "sex object" rather than as a highly competent person, you should dress for work in a conservative manner that suggests you are business-like. You should always be stylish and strive to dress as smartly as you would expect a lady to dress if she were a senior officer at a large bank or a partner in a CPA firm. Remember, your concern should always be business, not collecting boy friends.

Conclusion

Success and Sex don't mix. You may have been slightly disappointed with my suggestions in this chapter because they tell you what *not* to do rather than *what* to do and *how* to do it. But the cold, hard facts of life illustrate that many more careers have been ruined than aided by bringing sex to the office.

So that I don't ruin my own personal image, I do want to specify that I am certainly not trying to establish an antisex league. I enjoy sex and recognize the fact that it's definitely here to stay. I merely believe that you must keep it out of your career because it's far too dangerous when mixed with business. You must remember that your business has enough problems already; it doesn't need any more. Keeping the amorous part of your life separate from your career will help you build the winning image for which you are striving.

14 The Having-a-Sense-of-Humor Image

Having a good sense of humor is not only a strong plus in business, but it's also a sure way to make your career more enjoyable. A sense of humor will relieve tension and create the kind of relaxed atmosphere that will give you much added mileage in your career. It's also a winning-image builder, and will be reflected in the relationships you share with others, such as business associates, customers, and employees. Heed my Sense-of-Humor Principle: When given a choice, most people would rather deal with the individual who has a sense of humor.

In the past, perhaps because of early America's "work ethic," business and humor didn't mix. Americans believed that work was not to be associated with pleasure, and if a man didn't practically collapse by sundown, it was thought that he wasn't putting in an honest day's work. Our forefathers had their reasons for believing in such a philosophy, but over the years Americans have come to realize that work should be enjoyed. They've also come to believe that an individual is more productive if he finds his work pleasurable. Even our bankers have a more relaxed attitude today. In the past they were stuffed-shirt, pompous individuals who wore dark suits and never cracked a smile. Today's banker may still occasionally wear a dark suit, but he's definitely friendly and he's even permitted to have a sense of humor. In fact, it is now acceptable for everyone in American industry to have a sense of humor—even a funeral director may display one.

While businessmen are still as serious as ever about the "bottom line," they now do business with a smile, or even a grin. Rather than suggesting "softness," warmth actually demonstrates strength because it indicates confidence. Today's business is bigger and better than ever. Bankers now make loans considerably larger than those made in the past. Everything about business is done on a larger scale, and because of the competition in our business world, with more efficiency than ever before. For today's business and professional people, displaying this air of confidence through a sense of humor is definitely a winning image. Not everyone uses it, but those who don't are the unlucky ones.

When I speak of a sense of humor, I must stress that, like anything else, it must be put in its proper perspective. Most of the time a sense of humor can be a great ice-breaker, but in certain situations it can be out of place. Good judgment is necessary in determining when you should use it. Obviously, you can overdo it. For example, it's simply poor selling to approach a prospective customer, slap him on the back, and ask, "Say, ol' buddy, have you heard the joke about the traveling saleslady?" It's not that I'm opposed to telling a good joke, but timing does make a difference. You would not appreciate your attorney's jokes about bankruptcy if you were experiencing difficulties in your own business and were about to go under. Nor would your doctor's jokes seem too funny if you were lying in a hospital bed and being fed intravenously.

Many people in today's complex society are overwhelmed and frustrated by the system. Because stress and tension are more prevalent now than ever before, a good sense of humor is increasingly important. It is often just the right prescription to ease an otherwise hyper situation. If you're gifted with a good sense of humor, you should develop it, for it is definitely an excellent trait. People will appreciate working with you because of it.

Perhaps what we like most about the successful man who has a sense of humor is that he doesn't seem to take himself too seriously. How refreshing! The average person expects the man in a powerful position to be an egomaniac reeking with self-importance. He's usually pictured as overly vain and self-centered. "I can't get over it," declares Harvey Bristolcreme. "Walt Dizzy of Dizzy Enterprises is just a plain, ordinary guy. It's absolutely amazing," he tells his friends. "I had a meeting with one of the most important men in American business, and he's really no different than any one of us. Boy, I'll tell you, success didn't spoil Walt Dizzy. What a great, great guy!" Actually it was Walt Dizzy's aptitude for making the people around him feel comfortable that relaxed everyone who met him and gave people the impression he's "one of the boys."

It's always a surprise and a relief when people discover that successful individuals are basically no different from anyone else. The majority of people expect highly successful men and women to be very solemn and earnest because they make such big decisions. An executive who has a relaxed personality and good sense of humor leaves a favorable impression. You've undoubtedly often heard someone say, when discussing one of these tycoons, "I can identify with him." The party who makes the remark has absolutely nothing in common with the tycoon, but the relaxed atmosphere, not the man himself, becomes the means of identification.

Greeting someone with whom you are about to do business with a warm smile is the best way to introduce yourself. People can't help immediately liking such an individual. He seems humble, and they're impressed with his informal manner. They notice his "human side," and he wins them over at once. People *want* to do business with this kind of man. A friendly first meeting sets the stage beautifully for the formal discussions.

On the other hand, there's the humorless, dull type who turns you completely off. Stanley Shtick, president of a large grocery chain called Shtick's Foods, is a good example. "Stanley Shtick is the coldest fish I ever met," says Zelda Zoftik on her first meeting with him. "He's so damned pompous. You would think he was the King of England, the way he acts," she complains. "The longer it is before I meet with him again, the better."

Recently, watching a politician deliver a campaign speech, I was struck by the man's obvious lack of a sense of humor. He came across as completely dry, and seemed impressed with his own importance. In short, he was an absolute bore. This was unfortunate because, in my opinion, he is a brilliant man who has considerable talents. He has the necessary skills to do an outstanding job as an administrator, but as a leader who must relate to the people, he's a loser. Had his speech writers injected some subtle humor into his speech, he would have relaxed his audience, and they would have felt they could identify with him because he would have appeared more friendly and personable.

Another candidate, Clyde Hopper, is a man who possesses a delightful sense of humor. He comes up with the perfect quip no matter what group he is addressing. His audiences love him. When speaking to a group of big businessmen, he tells them, "In a society where everybody is a millionaire, I ought to be able to make a living," and they howl. He practically has them in his hip pocket. When speaking to a ladies' group, he tells the story about the person who suggested to him that he marry his opponent (he happens to be running against a female) for with her beauty and his brains, the pair might be able to create a "super" candidate. "But what if the offspring has her brains and my looks!" he quips. While this kind of humor may be nothing more than sheer amusement, people associate it with wit, and wit is associated with intelligence.

Not long ago, I attended a surprise party given for the president of a large insurance/financial holding company, at which both co-executives and good friends of the family were present. The "noncompany" guests were very favorably impressed by the closeness among the others. The good-natured roasting the guest of honor received from his fellow workers clearly indicated the kind of relationship he shares with them. If they didn't feel a special way toward him, they could never have gotten away with what would otherwise have been considered downright hostile remarks. The wonderful sense of humor he obviously displays at the office inspired in his guests the highest regard for both him and his executive team and admiration for the excellent *esprit de corps* they apparently enjoy.

The next time you go to a cocktail party, a convention, or any other large gathering where you shake hands with several people but never really engage in any serious conversation, make note of the people who impressed you the most. Even during brief introductions and a few minutes of conversation, you can distinguish those who have a sense of humor. They are the ones who are most radiant and charming; their attitude reveals their enjoyment of life, and it generates a cheerful winning image. Their sense of humor is bound to affect everyone with whom they come in contact.

Humor can frequently be just the right medicine for easing a tense situation. Dr. Balk's sense of humor seems to charm his patients. When self-pitying Kelly Grace moaned to him, "But Dr. Balk, I was looking forward to the most exciting time of my life—a two-week vacation in Italy—and now you insist that I must have my gallbladder removed!" the good doctor held her hand and softly said, "Look at it this way, my dear Kelly: a trip to Italy only lasts for two weeks, but a gallbladder removal lasts for a lifetime." As you can see, with a sense of humor you can put a seemingly serious problem in its proper perspective.

Van Trucks, president of Trucks and Trucks, Inc., makes use of his humor when dealing with his executives. A disgruntled junior executive approached Trucks with a frown and announced, "Mr. Trucks, my wife requested that I speak directly to you about the transfer to Pittsburgh which the company has planned for our family. She's very content living in Chicago and doesn't particularly want to move to Pittsburgh. While I'm certain that I can convince her the move is in the best interest of my career with the

"Don't be silly, Cecil. You've been with the company for thirty-one years, but that doesn't mean you have to share my sense of humor."

company, she asked me to speak to you about it to find out if the company had any options for us. She'll certainly agree with anything I do, but Pittsburgh—well, you know, it just doesn't turn her on. Naturally, I'm a company man, and I'll surely do what's best for Trucks and Trucks, but I promised her that I would talk to you, so here I am."

Trucks' warm smile assured the young executive that the company really understood his problem. "Lou," said Truck, "you tell your sweet wife Lois that she certainly does have a choice." He then put his arm on Lou's shoulder and continued, "She can either stay here in Chicago or go with you to Pittsburgh!" Lou laughed and responded, "By golly, that's exactly what I'll tell her."

Trucks then added, "Seriously, Lou, it's a wonderful opportunity for you, and I want you to believe that I know you and Lois will really enjoy Pittsburgh. It happens to be a great city. By the way, how about having lunch with me on Wednesday?"

Again, a sense of humor can create goodwill. Applying it to this kind of situation is definitely more gentle and appropriate than merely saying no to a dissatisfied employee.

Conclusion

Life is too short to tackle without a sense of humor. With it, you can place any seemingly large problem in its proper perspective and laugh about it. Getting others to join you makes the problem—and you—more approachable.

15 What's the Right Image for Me?

Ever since I began this book, I have been approached by people asking my advice in determining the right image for them. Naturally, I can't give any pat answers because, first of all, there's a great deal of information to be digested before deciding on the best image.

While making the TV circuit on various talk shows throughout the country in order to promote my book, *Total Commitment,* I was constantly asked if I was planning to write another book. I always answered that I was working on a manuscript entitled *Winning Images,* and then I briefly discussed a few of my ideas. Following one such talk show, I was cornered by Ty Knotts, a friendly, well-known TV personality who hosts an excellent talk show in the South. "Tell me, Bob," Ty inquired, "what's the best winning image for me? I've often wondered about this, so perhaps you can give me some advice."

"Ty," I replied, "I really don't know enough about you to make such a recommendation. Many factors have to be considered. The very first question you must answer is: 'What are my objectives?' Next, Ty, what image do *you* want to project? In your field, for example, you can be effective by coming across to your audience in several different ways. Do you want to be the sweet, lovable, nice guy—you know, the friendly, next-door-neighbor type—or do you want to be an entirely opposite type—the flamboyant TV celebrity? And, of course, there's the provocative type, and the highly sophisticated TV host. Ty, there are many, many ways you can go."

"Those are some mighty big choices, Bob," Ty drawled. "What's the answer?"

"I can't give you an on-the-spot answer, Ty. *You* are the one who has to make the decision. Of course, the kind of person you are will be the most significant factor in your decision because what you're really projecting with a TV image is your own personality." I paused and then said, "Ty, I really can't see you as the flamboyant or sophisticated type. Neither seems to be really you, and your audience down here probably wouldn't like you in either of those roles. You have to consider what image will wear well over a long period of time. In your field, it's easy for the audience to become fickle and get tired of a TV personality."

There is no simple clear-cut answer to such an important question. Perhaps my conversation with Ty Knotts will give you some idea of the complexities involved. Only after considering all pertinent factors will you be able to decide upon your winning image.

If you have contact with other people, you must be concerned with the image you project to them, no matter what your field. For instance, most people think a minister, priest, or rabbi has a built-in image that they come by naturally; but these men, too, must be concerned with a winning image. A clergyman must ask himself the same kind of questions I asked Ty Knotts. Like a TV personality, he also has an audience. Of course, the clergyman's image isn't limited to his pulpit, for he must also be concerned with how he comes across on a one-to-one basis in private meetings with different members of his congregation.

At the same time, he must think about his image with the church's board. He has a responsibility to the entire community, and with the right winning image, he can be one of its most influential citizens. Each man may have his own different style, but all can be equally effective. I know a very dedicated minister whose warmth radiates to all those with whom he comes in contact. Another friend of mine, a very learned rabbi, has an opposite personality. By nature, he's a cold person, and he comes across as regal. Unlike the minister, he remains aloof from the members of his congregation. Yet the rabbi is a very positive influence, not only on the members of his congregation, but on the entire city in which he lives.

There is a good lesson to be learned from the experience of a young minister, Reverend Kidd, who inherited the congregation of Reverend Lord, after Lord's unexpected death from a heart attack. Reverend Lord had been with the congregation for more than thirty years, and it should have been obvious to all that no one could ever take his place. Unfortunately, the young Reverend Kidd tried to emulate the deceased clergyman in the belief that by doing so he would be more readily accepted by the congregation. This decision proved to be a serious mistake, and I spoke with him about it a few months later. "Reverend Kidd," I said, "let's face reality. You're never going to have the personality Reverend Lord had. So quit trying to be *him!* If you don't, you'll only be, at best, a second-rate Reverend Lord. Instead, be a first-rate Reverend Kidd." Not long after, Reverend Kidd began to be himself and was soon accepted by the congregation. I believe that someday, in his own way, he'll be as much loved and cherished as was the late Reverend Lord.

You, too, will make a serious mistake if you take over a position held by a very popular predecessor and attempt to copy his or her personality. Instead, *be yourself.* Project your own image, not the other fellow's, because you'll never come across the way he did no matter how hard you try. I don't care whether you're the president of a large corporation who's brought in from another company, a schoolteacher, a new sales manager, a military officer, or a new coach. You must not attempt to be an exact replica of the person whom you are replacing. People don't expect you to, nor do they particularly want you to. Each successor must project his or her own winning image as an individual, not as an imitation of the person who formerly had the job.

Pat Bottoms, an acquaintance of mine, was recently named vice president in charge of marketing for a large insurance company, Executive Mutual Life Insurance Company. Previously, Pat had done a most commendable job with another company that specialized in selling hospitalization insurance. He had been a great motivator of his former agents and had run weekly and monthly sales contests in which the winners received such inexpensive prizes as portable radios, neckties, and cheap watches. His unlimited expense account had allowed him to wine and dine his men at fine restaurants throughout his territory. He had always ordered expensive steak dinners for them and before the night was over he and the agents were usually bombed. The unsophisticated hospitalization agents loved Bottoms for his "buddy-buddy" personality. He was, as he told them, one of the boys and always in their corner. When Bottoms went to Executive Mutual, he tried to use the same techniques with a highly sophisticated sales force. These agents weren't too impressed when he took them out to paint the town and they didn't appreciate his swinger image. They wanted a sales manager who could provide them with product knowledge, not one who could outdrink them. They wanted sales ideas and follow-up, not cheap watches. Unfortunately, Bottoms wasn't able to relate to his new sales force, and he soon found himself unemployed. The winning image he'd enjoyed in one "market" turned out to be just a dud in another.

Just as the individual must develop his or her own identity, so must every product and every company. I think the first major question to be asked before attempting to build your company's right winning image is: "What am I after?" Unless you're General Motors or Federated Department Stores, you must realize that you can't have something for everybody all the time. Only giant corporations sometimes enjoy such a position. The vast majority of businesses must identify their market. A small clothing store, for example, can't be expected to have a full line of clothing for men, women, and children, or offer merchandise ranging in quality from the lowest to the highest, as large department stores so often do. Such a retailer must therefore decide what kind of store he wishes to operate. Does he wish to sell to the masses or cater to the carriage trade? Over the past ten years I have noticed that retailers who have become specialists in a particular area are the most successful. Once they develop a winning formula for a local area, they apply it in many markets across the country and soon build their businesses into successful national operations. These businesses develop a winning image because they specialize in one segment of a large market and don't try to have something for everyone.

A good example of what I *don't* mean is the restaurant we've all seen (and laughed at) that tries to attract all customers with ads such as We Specialize in Chinese-Italian-Jewish Foods. It seems they're afraid they'll lose business if the wife wants eggroll, the husband craves pizza, and the kid wants a kosher corned beef sandwich. In my opinion, the public will most likely think, "They can't be good at preparing any of those foods." Such an attitude decreases, rather than increases, business. Equally bad is the restaurant with a flashing neon sign on the front of the building that simply reads: Food, Food. If you study the successes of local restaurants in your own area and those that have expanded into large, national chains, you'll discover that specialization distinguishes the successful ones, whether they be hamburger stands or famous French restaurants.

The Specialization Principle is also applicable in the operation of an employment agency. Karl Klutz, the owner of Klutz & Klutz Employment Agency, thinks that he should be able to have enough applicants available to fill any position that any company has open. He doesn't like to let a prospective employee out of his office without having some sort of job for him or her, so he advertises: Klutz & Klutz Has a Job for Everyone; You Name It and We'll Get It for You! In theory, this sounds great, but in actual practice, it's not possible to maintain a competitive edge against the many other employment agencies that specialize. Since Klutz & Klutz isn't strong in any

particular market, business has been on a downward
trend during the past several years, even though, at
one time, they were the largest employment - agency
in town. Their competition specializes in such areas as
the computer, the secretarial, and the transportation
fields, and, of course, there are the "headhunters" who
specialize in relocating top executives.

Even a product such as beer, which can be consumed by an individual of any social standing, must
have an image that will appeal to a certain market.
Some beers gear their advertising to the working man,
while others go after the upper-income market. Moor
Beer is an outstanding example of a product that has
had phenomenal success throughout the Southwest because its brewers have developed a winning image
for it by advertising it as the choice of the elite. Their
advertising campaigns show only highly successful
people drinking Moor Beer and celebrities requesting
"Moor Beer, please." These ads are accompanied by a
song with lyrics about Moor Beer being only for the
beer drinker who's discriminating. The next time
you're in the Southwest, notice how many "in-the-
know" Moor beer drinkers act when they order "Moor
Beer, please." Drinking this beer has definitely become
a status symbol, although I seriously doubt that its
taste is different from that of other beers.

Every shopping center or land developer must appreciate the value of a winning image. When developing a shopping center, for example, the owners must
decide on a "theme" and then solicit leases according
to the market they plan to cater to. The shopping
center that takes every tenant just to fill up empty
stores as quickly as possible will soon reach a point
where it is only half filled and unable to attract any
more tenants. With a theme, however, different stores
will attract the same type of customers, so each retailer

"Add a few more angels, and you'll have just the right winning image I want."

will generate traffic for others because they complement one another. A developer of a new suburban community must also decide which market he wishes to attract. He can't, for example, build expensive homes on one block and cheap two-family homes on the next. He must plan the size of lots as well as the style of homes so that they complement rather than detract from one another.

Conclusion

Many other examples could be given to emphasize my point but I think the message is clear: *You must know what market you're after before you attempt to develop the right image.* Knowing this is the basis for beginning anything. You can't get anywhere until you have a destination, or, in the case of an image, a goal.

As an individual trying to establish a winning image, you must analyze your personality and then coordinate it to fit the image you desire. As a businessman, you must consider the resources so that you don't bite off more than you can chew. As your business grows, you can then make whatever adjustments seem necessary to develop a long-range, bigger image. Many large department stores started with only a pushcart, and large manufacturing companies often began in a small shop in the founder's garage. The important thing to remember is that you must *know* the value of a winning image, and then decide on the one you want.

16 Losing Images

I don't think it would be possible to write a book on winning images without including a chapter on losing images. After all, our idea of winning is relative to what we believe is "losing."

As I mentioned in the introduction, never be insincere in your efforts to project an image. The phony image will sooner or later be exposed for what it is, and when this happens, you'll be plagued with a losing image that is far worse then remaining obscure. You can safely conclude that no image is better than a losing one.

Tru Blue, the swinger in "A Chapter on Sex," is a good example of a person with a losing image. Once his swinging image catches up with him, he'll rue the day he ever looked at a nice pair of legs during his working hours. Amazingly, however, many men and women want to project the image of "being cool," even though they should have outgrown such behavior upon graduating from high school. I maintain that if you want to be perceived this way socially, you should keep this kind of image separate from your work because such an image doesn't do a thing for your career.

I am not suggesting that you should in any way attempt to project a pompous image. The opposite of the swinger image is equally objectionable. We've all seen the individual who looks down on someone's behavior if there is the slightest reason to doubt his actions. Behaving as if you were a saint does not impress very many people.

There's also the person who thinks he's just too damned good to mingle with anyone other than the bluebloods of the community. Dan DeLyons is the vice president of an exclusive ladies' department store, Boyce and Mann. When his father retires, Dan will be president. Anybody who ever met DeLyons would think he was next in line for the throne of England. Not only does he refuse to acknowledge his employees by their names, but he never says "Good morning" unless he's spoken to first. He's a completely different person, however, when the wife of one of the members of his country club comes to Boyce and Mann to shop. DeLyons is all personality with his friends. He shuns only the "common people," such as his employees and the salesmen who call on him. What a miserable way to work with people! Not only is such behavior in poor taste, but it's a very ineffective way to get results. Nothing can be accomplished with this kind of attitude, but much can be lost. Because of the poor morale of its employees, it is easy to understand why Boyce and Mann has a high labor turnover.

A similar type is the person who believes he is better than people who are below him socially or economically. His attitude is that looking down on others creates a winning image because it compels others to look up to him. Little does he realize that *nobody* respects such an individual. Phil Morris, a savings and loan president who has worked hard to create such an image, mingles with his employees, but his favorite pastime when with them is to drop the names of personal friends who, in his view, are the pillars of the community. He isn't above taking one of his vice presidents to his clubs, but when he does, his favorite conversation, in an effort to impress his guest, is how much money each of his friends has. Phil can't be very good company when he takes you to his exclusive city club, The City Square Club, because he's either looking around to see who else is there or jumping from table to table shaking everyone's hand while his guest sits staring at his plate or looking off into space. Everybody who has ever gone to lunch with him dreads a second experience. His wife Phyllis is also adept at making her "inferiors" (this includes most people) feel very uncomfortable. Remarkably, however, the personalities of both husband and wife completely change when they are around people they consider important. What a difference a few million dollars makes!

Nick Nack, the founder and president of a large trucking company, projects an image opposite to that of Phil Morris, yet it is equally obnoxious. Since he worked his way up after starting with just one truck, Nick's favorite conversation is about how he started from scratch and is now one of the wealthiest men in town. If someone mentions another successful person's name, Nick will tell him, "That Dan DeLyons never had to worry about where his next meal was coming from. His grandfather was quite a man but DeLyons can't make a living on his own." Or, after Phil Morris leaves his table at the club, Nick will turn to his luncheon guest and say, "When I was poor, that bastard would never say hello to me. Now that I'm important and rich, I can't keep the guy away from me." And if the name of another self-made man pops up, Nick will comment, "That son of a bitch is the luckiest guy I ever met. It's incredible that a guy like him can even make a living, let alone be worth millions. There's a perfect example of a man being at the right place at the right time!"

Nick Nack also tries to impress everyone with his blatant generosity. "Don't give him the fish," he orders the waitress as he slaps her on the backside, "Give him the steak. The big one. And the best wine you've got. Money's no object! My associate and I want only the best!" And, whether hungry or completely stuffed, you'd better leave room for dessert because Nick Nack is going to order it for you. It seems as though he's trying to win a prize for running up the biggest bill in town.

While you should never try to cut corners when entertaining, nobody appreciates seeing you throw your money around as if it's going out of style. I seriously doubt if anyone is overly impressed when you give the headwaiter a $20 tip just to get a good table. The same holds true for the attention you give the wine steward, the maitre d', and the waitress. If you're trying to impress a customer, he's likely to think, "Boy, they must really be making a huge profit on the business they do with us. Perhaps I'd better shop around with some competitors to see if we can work out a closer deal." And if you're dining with one of your salesmen or employees, he might think, "Instead of blowing this money on liquor and food, I think I'll ask for a raise and tell him I'll go out to eat by myself." In other words, your efforts may backfire, and the money you're spending produce negative results.

Another poor image projected by many large corporations is having "executive restrooms." I could never understand why a class distinction is made for the use of the toilet. While having the "right" to use the executive restroom may be a status symbol for those executives who have earned their keys, it has to have a poor effect on the individual who hasn't yet won the honor of using the exclusive john!

Equally bad is having parking spaces reserved for executives of the company. I have always been under the impression that the higher-echelon managers were the first to arrive at work so they automatically got the best parking spaces. Those people who arrived later ended up with less desirable spaces. In my opinion, the only reserved parking spaces should be those used by the handicapped. In all other situations, it should be first come, first served.

When I am asked what I think about executive dining rooms, I usually respond with a question: "What's the purpose of such segregation?" If a great number of outsiders visit the company, then setting up separate dining areas for the executives and their frequent guests can be effective. However, if the intent is merely to separate the management from the rest of the company, this arrangement will be damaging because it will hurt the morale of those who aren't permitted in the special dining area. According to what I've seen, only very few executive dining areas are worth the expense.

For those of you who enjoyed my chapter on intimidation, let me add that if you don't use discretion, such tactics will surely backfire on you. I do not approve of the kind of intimidation whereby you browbeat the next guy until he's senseless. If you're going to use intimidation, please be very subtle about it, because it can be effective only when used in moderation. Don't be like Frank Stein, the chief operating officer of Frank N. Stein, Inc., who tells his employees, "Look, I'm the only one in this company who is authorized to think. When I give you an order, *you* don't think about it. I've never made a mistake in my life, and you're to do exactly as I command." He really thinks he knows how to motivate his employees when he shouts at them, "I expect every person who works for me to live in constant fear. It will make you perform. It's the greatest motivator there is." Perhaps you find it hard to believe that there are people in this world who actually treat their employees in this manner, but they *do* exist. Not only do they make people around them despise them, but inwardly, they must be miserable themselves. Nobody is really motivated by being pushed; instead, you must pull.

Another losing image is projected by the salesman who calls on a customer and, when asked a question, replies, "Look, I can't give you an answer for that one, but I'll check it out and let you know when I have an answer." We've all heard salesmen respond in this way, and they think they are being sincere in doing so. It's inexcusable, however, for a salesman to be so unprepared. His job is to know everything there is to know about his company and product, and failure to give complete answers when occupying another person's time is a form of disrespect. Many salesmen make this mistake, but *professional* salesmen don't.

"Playing dumb" is also a losing image. Newton Figg, a shrewd coal-stripping contractor from West Virginia, likes to tell people, "Look, I'm just a dumb hillbilly from the backwoods of good old West Virginia." When he's negotiating a large seven-figure loan from a New York banker, I seriously doubt that anybody really appreciates Figg's act. As a matter of fact, with a net worth that runs to eight figures, he's not fooling anyone. The "dumb blonde" type is no better. I advise all women to avoid such an act because it rarely deceives anyone. And those who are deceived really

"Oh, your financial statement is fine. There's just something about your losing image that pisses me off."

believe you're dumb—in which case, what do you have to gain?

Always be wary of the man who tells you, "Look, I'm telling you the absolute truth now." Whenever a person makes such a statement to me, I always start wondering about what he's told me previously! Is he really saying, "Well, okay, I lied to you, but now I'm being honest"?

Conclusion

Countless other losing images could be listed, but a quick review of other chapters will clearly indicate what they are. For example, in line with the discussion in the chapter on appearances and first impressions, you can surely imagine the reception a salesman would receive if he wore a plaid sport jacket and striped pants! The same holds true for the salesman who has a weak self-image and feels compelled to apologize, "Look, I can see you may be busy, Mr. Goodman, so, if you are, there's the door—just throw me out, and I'll stop back again whenever it's convenient for you." Though having a sense of humor is a winning image, there's certainly no place in business for the practical joker. By this time, I hope you also understand why it's a losing image if your wife serves Sloppy Joes when entertaining your business associates. Using plastic throwaway knives and forks, even though they do save time when cleaning up after a party, will project this same image.

Perhaps this chapter will serve as an eye-opener for you because, just as a winning image can get good results, a losing image can destroy you. Recognizing a losing image will certainly help you to appreciate a winning one. Since, as I said earlier, everybody will have an image sooner or later, why not have a winning one?

17 An Image or a Mirage?

There is a distinct difference between a winning image and a mirage. A mirage is an illusion, and in your quest for a winning image, you must be capable of identifying such mirages.

One of the most common misread images stems from what people think about eye contact. How many times have you heard, "You can tell he's an honest man because he looks you straight in the eye." Evidently, many people must believe that a dishonest man feels so ashamed that he's not telling the truth that he can't even face them directly. But what about an honest individual who is too shy to look straight at you? Furthermore, a good con artist knows that many people judge integrity by the way one looks at them, so he deliberately includes eye contact in his act. Because you can't count on eye contact as an infallible test, you should never use it to evaluate another person's honesty. Nonetheless, since most people *do* judge others by this criterion, be sure that *you* always look them squarely in the eye.

Evaluating a man's honesty by the way he looks at you makes no more sense than judging his integrity by the way your dog or cat reacts to him. Yet how many times have you heard a dog's master say, "That's interesting—Thor doesn't take to strangers very often. He's a good judge of human nature, and the fact that he's friendly with you tells me some good things about you." Once when I was in the home of a prospect, his cat, Tiger, took such a liking to me that he sat on my shoulder during my entire sales presentation. When I was finished, my prospect's wife said, "Mr. Shook, Tiger only does that with members of our immediate family. You must be a very honest person for her to be so friendly to you."

The truth of the matter was that I had refrained from pushing the cat off because I was afraid she'd rip my suit or scratch my eyes out. However, I replied, "Yes, ma'am, Tiger obviously has some kind of instinct that enables her to accurately judge humans. She sure is a good judge of character." Even though Tiger happened to be right in my case, I personally put very little faith in an animal's instinctual ability to judge people. I'd say his reactions have more to do with odors and body movement.

Some people judge another person by the way he or she shakes hands. A good, strong grip represents character, while a "dead-fish" handshake is a bad sign. I, too, dislike the flabby handshake with no life to it, but I am careful not to use it as a basis for judging an individual. Again, it's too easy for a con artist to put a hearty handshake into his act. Though *you* should give a firm handshake so you'll immediately create a good impression, don't place too much weight on the next fellow's grip; it doesn't tell you anything concrete about him.

There's a certain clean-cut appearance that creates

an honest image. For example, a blond, blue-eyed young man with a boyish grin and a look that typifies the boy-next-door, All-American type will almost always inspire confidence in others. There is no logical reason for placing such blind faith in a man simply because of the way he looks, yet most people do make such quick judgments. Conversely, the seedy man with dark oily skin, greasy black hair, and a moustache is not considered honest-looking. Similarly, a woman may have the looks which are usually associated with those of a streetwalker, whereas a high-priced call girl may look refined and refreshing. Naturally, clothes and—in the case of women—cosmetics have a great deal to do with such aforementioned appearances, but unfortunately a person's natural looks, over which he or she has little control, play an important part in the judgments most people will make. I pity the hardworking, honest salesman who was born with the looks that make people automatically think, "He's not the kind of man I'd want to buy a used car from!" On the other hand, a very devious individual may *look* like the type you can trust. How can you be sure that the hitchhiker who looks so clean-cut is any less dangerous than the one who, because of his appearance, looks like a risk? And how can you be sure that this one really *is* a risk? The point is that we are most often being completely unreasonable in making such snap decisions.

On a larger scale, voters often react favorably to a politician simply because of his clean-cut appearance. His opponent is often judged negatively because he has not been blessed with natural looks that generate trust. This kind of judgment is erroneous, and the consequences can produce devastating results. Granted, many people vote for a candidate strictly because of political issues, but the clean-cut image can tip the scales in favor of the wrong man in a close election.

We make snap judgments about people on the basis of how they express themselves. To revert to politics, many voters judge a candidate's ability by the way he makes a public speech. But though a candidate may be an effective speaker, he may not be capable of doing the job for which he is running. I know many highly talented men who simply have not developed an ability to speak well in public, but who are excellent in communicating with others on a one-to-one basis. The ability to express yourself strongly is always important, but we are too often wrongly impressed by the man who comes across as eloquent, since it is always possible that this virtue is only "skin deep." Yet it is easy to imagine a politician with a clean-cut look and a magnetic speaking voice romping all over his unassuming but better qualified opponent. He wins solely because his image is convincing.

After many years of interviewing and hiring salesmen, I have reached the conclusion that the man with the glib tongue doesn't necessarily become the top producer. Though there is a definite advantage in having a "natural" selling personality, more often than not the salesman with good working habits, proper motivation, and commitment is the one who becomes the best in his company. Too often, the sales manager who hires salesmen simply because of their extroverted and flamboyant personalities will have a high turnover.

Another influencing factor, which was discussed in the chapter "What's in a Name?" is the effect produced on the listener by the sound of a name. At some time or another, we've all been guilty of hastily forming an unwarranted opinion when we hear a "winning name" as opposed to a "losing" one. Hollywood recognized this fact long ago when the studios began changing the stars' real names. One of my favorite movie lines is James Bond's response to Pussy Galore, the heroine in the movie *Goldfinger*. Meeting her for the first time, he can only exclaim, "I must be dreaming!" Had her name been Harriett Finkelstein, the audience would never have been able to appreciate one of the screen's all-time great names! Yet, no matter how great a name is, using it as a criterion in evaluating character is just as illogical as determining a person's value by a handshake.

The beautiful, sexy redhead isn't always the best bed partner, nor is the big, strong man, whom we usually expect to be the hero, always braver than the small, frail man on the battlefield. Likewise, there is no sound reason for believing that the out-of-town attorney or consultant is any more of an expert than the local man. Just because your dentist has to book you six months in advance does not automatically mean that he does the best root-canal work. Nor will the insurance agent who drives a Mercedes necessarily give you better service than the agent who drives a Ford sedan. Having to go through a main switchboard, a receptionist, and a private secretary before you get to speak with your attorney is no indication of his legal abilities. I also hope you don't withdraw all your savings from Fourth Bank and deposit them with Third Bank just because their new home office building is several stories taller. It is equally unreasonable to assume that a hospital-clean restaurant serves the best food. True, all these factors are nice window dressing, and they shouldn't be completely ignored, but other more important factors must be considered before you make any final decisions about those with whom you'll do business.

"Oh, that's only a mirage. Great American is in Chapter 11."

Conclusion

Many images are only mirages that we have been conditioned to accept as the real thing. So don't be fooled the next time somebody tells you that Truman Blue is a great guy because of his wonderful smile, the way he looks people straight in the eye when he talks to them, his firm handshake, and his remarkable rapport with pets!

Building a Winning Image

Many people think it is difficult to build a winning image because there are no identifiable standards by which they can measure the results of their efforts. The intangible quality of image-building does not permit you to grasp anything concrete on a day-to-day basis, but in the long run, tangible results will definitely be evident.

If you are one of those people who is overly concerned about the intangible quality of image-building, let me remind you that many of the products and services you are very familiar with are also intangible. Yet their value is evident. For example, a successful salesman who sells a product such as insurance, education, securities, or mutual funds knows how to create need, even though the prospect can't actually see or touch what he is buying. Consequently, you must realize that *knowing* how to get results is what's really important. By now you should understand enough about winning

174

images to learn how to build one. You'll soon discover that you can accomplish outstanding results if you know *what* you want and *how* to get it. Once you reach this point, you must establish obtainable goals and then commit yourself to achieving them.

Perhaps my own experience in building a winning image will help you to relate to the process. Please keep in mind that when my father and I started our business fifteen years ago, we had very limited capital, and we were selling an intangible product. And even though we now have a winning image from coast to coast, we never spent any money on advertising (I firmly believe "it pays to advertise," but in our particular case we chose not to). Today, our company, Shook Associates Corporation, is considered one of the finest professional sales organizations in our industry.

I can honestly say that we were able to accomplish a great deal in a very short period of time primarily because we were so aware of building a winning image from the first day we started our business. Prior to that time, we had spent hundreds of hours discussing he image we desired. We committed ourselves by writing down the exact image we wanted, as well as what we would have to do to get it. As you can see, our winning image didn't come about by accident, and our growth, unusually rapid for our industry, stemmed directly from our image-building efforts. Furthermore, our growth and image-building occurred simultaneously, and complemented each other: The image helped us to become successful, and the success helped build our image.

We were concerned with four specific images, all of which influenced others. First, we recognized that we had to have a quality product of outstanding value to our client. We knew that without a winning product, a sales organization could never be built on a strong foundation. This is true of any business. No matter how hard you work at it, you must offer a product or service that will benefit your customers. If you fail to do this, you'll constantly be fighting an uphill battle, and you'll eventually lose. Finding a product of legitimate value is not really difficult. Most companies have one or they wouldn't be in business (unless, of course, they're con artists, and are trying to build on a clay foundation).

The next image we sought was a professional reputation with our clients. We needed their faith in us so that they would refer us to other prospects *because we were good at what we did*. Only by offering better service could we accomplish this, so, naturally, we were committed to follow up on anything we promised. By developing a very comprehensive sales presentation and putting together an effective training program, we were able to put men in the field who generated confidence in their prospects because they came across as professional salesmen. The men were trained to handle any sales situation.

Of course, in order to develop a highly professional sales organization, we had to recruit quality salesmen. Only by being ultraselective were we able to eventually develop a sales force that would project the winning image we were after. We rejected many applicants, even though they would have been top producers, simply because we felt they weren't the type who would help us achieve the long-range professional image we wanted. Because we disciplined ourselves to pass up this kind of salesman, we were able to accomplish the winning image which we now enjoy. Certainly, it's always very tempting to make an extra dollar when you first begin a business, but sometimes you'll pay for it many times over in the future.

Phil Fine, a long-time acquaintance of my father, is

a good example of the type of salesman we had to reject. When we first began our company, Phil was eager to represent us. He was a struggling home-improvement salesman at the time, but his past work experiences included selling used cars, Florida real estate (mostly underwater properties, as it turned out), and magazines door to door. While we could have permited Phil to represent us on straight commission, and therefore lose nothing by giving him an opportunity for old times' sake, he would have been a liability in out attempts to attract other quality salesmen, for they could easily have thought, "If Shook Associates would consider hiring Phil Fine, they must be desperate for salesmen. There must be something wrong with the job if they can't attract top men." Our philosophy was that any job easy to get must have something wrong with it. Thus, if we had unattractive, unpolished men representing us, we would quickly develop a losing, rather than winning, image. Our choice to pass on Phil Fine and many others like him in the early stages of our career eventually paid handsome dividends because being selected by Shook Associates became that much more desirable.

The final image we had to build was from within. In order to motivate our associates, we had to be in a position to offer them excellent opportunities for advancement. This is a very important consideration for any company with growth aspirations. *You only grow with people,* and in order to attract and keep quality people, you must be willing to give them an opportunity to share in your future successes. If your people find that they don't have this opportunity, your company will suffer from low morale and high turnover of personnel. If either occurs, you've reached the end of the road, and unless you're willing to make some major changes, it's going to be a downhill journey.

Even more important is the fact that we constantly credited our "system," rather than our personal talents, with our success. While it may have been more flattering to our egos to tell our people how great we were when our company reached certain plateaus and achieved sales records, we always told them that the credit should go to established Shook Associates procedures, not to us personally. The reason for convincing them of the value of our system was that we wanted them to know that they, too, would be successful if they accepted our guidelines. We didn't want them to think, "Sure, Bob and Herb can do it, but nobody else can." After all, what good would it have done to convince them of our own excellence—they had to believe *they* could do it.

As mentioned earlier, we had a master plan of simultaneously building four images (product, service, quality people, and opportunity for advancement), which all complemented one another. For example, without a quality product, we couldn't attract quality salesmen. Without quality salesmen, we couldn't adequately present our product in a top professional way. And without advancement opportunities for our salesmen, we wouldn't be able to keep our people motivated. Most important, our image-building process stemmed from a pre-planned scheme. We didn't just go about selling insurance with the dream that someday we'd hire other salesmen. We carefully plotted how we were going to build a winning image in order to accomplish our goals.

I also want to emphasize that while our business grew, we constantly made adjustments in our image-building. Being flexible in your image-building is very important; whenever necessary you should make changes along the way. This is true in respect to every facet of building a business; you should never become so rigid that you refuse to bend and sway when necessary. You must always consider factors such as economic conditions, differences among people in varying parts of the country, differences among your own people, and changing lifestyles.

Similarly, you must constantly inject new techniques and ideas into your image-building campaign. Over the years, we continually updated our sales presentation, our selling techniques, and our corporate structure. Doing so enabled us to be competitive in attracting salesmen and people for sales management. For example, we made many changes in our recruiting brochures, and when our book, *How to Be the Complete Professional Salesman,* was published, we naturally added it to our recruiting arsenal. I must confess we played the book to the hilt. When a prospective agent came in for an interview, he would be told, "Shook Associates offers you the finest opportunity in America for a career in professional selling. Some companies merely go through the motions of selling, and their salesmen make a mediocre living. Other companies develop professional salesmen, and these salesmen are the highest paid professionals in the world. We're one of those companies. In fact, our management wrote *the* book on professional selling."

At this point, the recruitee was given a copy of *How to Be the Complete Professional Salesman.* As pointed out in Chapter 6, we felt that doing so doubled our effectiveness in hiring salesmen, for the book was not only a tangible object the man himself could see and hold, but something he could take home to his wife, who also had to be sold on our company. Though I am not suggesting that you write a book in order to recruit salesmen, I do urge you to make every effort to give a prospect something tangible. An attractive printed brochure—perhaps with illustrations—that explains your company would be excellent. The brochures could very possibly be expensive but, as is true of any other business proposition, you must consider the value you'll receive in exchange for the cost.

As our company grew, we were able to do many other things to build the winning image we were after. A few years ago, we came out with a company monthly newsletter. (The newsletter, if done properly, can be one of your most effective image-builders.) As mentioned in the chapter, "The Stability Principle," we soon built our own office building, an expensive but very effective image-builder. We hosted sales conventions in Florida and in the exotic Caribbean, and had frequent management meetings for our executive team in equally desirable places. We either went first class or not at all. We never tried to cut down by staying at cheaper hotels (we would rather shorten the trip by a day), nor did we try to save on meals. We wanted our people to have the best time of their lives, and I believe that most of them actually did. We truly appreciated our people for their fine performances, and we wanted them to know how much they meant to us.

Being selective was our key to attracting top men, and keeping them highly motivated was our method of retaining them. It didn't take long for a new man to realize that we were not only a company with extreme integrity, but one completely loyal to its sales force as well. Because of this, they responded to us with the same kind of integrity and loyalty. We stressed the importance of having a good appearance, and we fully prepared our people to represent us in the field like professional salesmen. Since the salesman is, in most cases, the company's only personal contact with the prospect, we wanted to be positive that our representatives would create a winning image for our company.

This they did and the quality of the people who represented us as well as the quality of the product we sold soon increased our company's prestige immeasurably. As I said, we put together a package of four images, and each complemented the other.

Another very effective image-builder was my second book, *Total Commitment*, which is based on the theory that total commitment is fundamental to great achievements. It is the motivation that drives men to succeed. In order to prove this hypothesis, my co-author and I interviewed twenty highly successful Americans in such diverse fields as business, sports, entertainment, medicine, public service, and science. The persons interviewed included: John W. Galbreath, a prominent real estate developer; Kemmons Wilson, chairman of Holiday Inns; Edgar Speer, chairman of U.S. Steel Corporation; Willard Rockwell, Jr., chairman of Rockwell International; Kingman Brewster, president of Yale University; Pete Rose; Sam Snead; Denton Cooley, M.D.; Jesse Owens; Alan King; and Hugh Downs. We devoted an entire chapter to each person interviewed and the information and philosophies they gave us. Because of the exposure the book gave us, it was an excellent means for building the image of our company. I was interviewed on dozens of TV and radio stations, and by newspapers and magazines, and, as a consequence, my name and that of our company received great publicity. Further, because of my personal interviews with some of America's greatest achievers, I was often regarded as being "one of them." I realize I don't belong in their league, but the celebrity status I enjoyed certainly helped our winning image!

My sister, Lois Becker, has also done an excellent job in building an image for her career. She is a splendid artist, now living in Cleveland. There are many fine artists in this world, all of whom possess enough talent to produce quality work, but I believe their inability to develop a winning image keeps them from becoming successful. A good number are only barely able to put food on their tables. My point is that judgment of art is relative, dependent on individual taste, and the reception the artist receives from the public is more likely than not based on his or her image. After all, when a painting of a tin can or a red square inside a black circle can command a price tag higher than the average American family's annual income, the artist's image must play a strong role in determining the value of the work in question.

Lois, an art major who graduated from Chatham College, and the mother of two children, began to support her family when her husband was going to medical school. She's been working hard as an artist ever since, for almost twenty years. Lois is quite talented, but I sincerely believe that her ability to build a winning image enabled her to excel in her field. After all, it's one thing to paint an object on canvas, and it's quite another thing to be able to sell it! In a field in which success is difficult and competition is paramount, Lois has developed another important talent—she knows how to merchandise her work. Most of her promotion is based solely on her winning image. Early in her career, being particular about where she displayed her work prevented both overexposure and the losing image that comes from being exhibited with inferior art. Like any other struggling artist, she wanted to sell her work, but she was smart enough to avoid second-rate art promotions in shopping centers, amateur art shows, high schools, churches, and similar places. Lois was also adamant about how much her paintings were worth and she refused to bargain with a customer who offered her a lower price. She felt that if he wasn't willing to pay her price, he wasn't worthy of owning her work! While she might have lost a few sales in the short run, she more than made up for them over the years.

As Lois prospered, she contacted leading art galleries throughout the city and later throughout the eastern part of the United States, to ask them to exhibit her art. An excellent sales person, she did a fine job of convincing them to do business wtih her. She was a refreshing change of pace from the hippie image most artists have in the popular mind. She always dressed like a lady, and her beauty made it a pleasure to do business with her. Today, Lois makes jewelry and is the author of a book entitled *How to Make and Sell Your Arts and Crafts*. Each of Lois' three projects complement one another. She lectures many times each year and, being the creator of fine art and beautiful jewelry, as well as an author, convinces people that she is very talented.

Lois has also appeared on TV and radio talk shows in many cities throughout the country. In addition, many feature articles have been written about her art, her jewelry, and her book. Because of this exposure she has become well known, and this has allowed her to demand higher prices for her creations. It really doesn't matter whether she is interviewed on her book, her jewelry, or her art because she's promoting *Lois Becker*. Having her name in the limelight sells her products!

Because many fine artists have no regard for building a winning image, they allow their image to be determined strictly by fate. They want only to create art, and will live a life of obscurity—unless someone else decides to promote their work (and their image).

Another good example of image-building is the case of Melody Singer, a gal from Nashville who wants to make it as a country singer. I recently spent a few hours in Nashville trying to give Melody some tips on how she could develop her image, but I'm afraid I was wasting both her time and mine. She is very talented, but she's been using a part-time agent (who's also a full-time barber) to promote her. Melody's engagements are usually in small cities within a five-state area, normally in places such as Holiday Inns, Ramada Inns, and similar small nightclub-restaurants. I suggested that she contact each city's newspapers and local TV and radio talk shows so that she could be interviewed and get extra publicity during the mornings and afternoons while she's on the road; or if she's too shy to promote herself, she should have her agent do it. Over a period of time, I explained, she would become a "celebrity" in these cities because of this kind of local-media exposure. It would really be very easy for someone like Melody to become a guest on talk shows, since they need such people in order to survive. Unbelievably, the thought of contacting the media had never occurred to Melody's agent. (I do understand, however, that he gives a very good haircut!) I told Melody she should get an experienced agent, for she was ruining her chances of success by using an amateur to promote her. This recommendation offended her and she told me that her loyalty to the agent/barber would never allow her to replace him. When I told her that she was working on borrowed time (she's thirty-four years old and still "undiscovered"), and had better make a big move soon before her looks disappear, she again felt insulted.

Melody has made two records, both of which did moderately well. Each is on the same subject—CB radio songs. The reason I had arranged our meeting was to convince her to record a third song about CB radios, one a friend of mine and I had written. She

"In line with my image-building program, I want the people of my kingdom to be known throughout the world as the most highly educated citizens of any nation. I hereby decree that each and every one of you be granted a Ph.D."

liked the song, but she told me, "I just don't want to do it without the permission of my agent." I could understand her not wanting to make the decision on her own, and asked her to call me in the morning to let me know what the agent had decided. When she called, she said, "Bob, we both love your song, but he doesn't want me to get a CB-radio image. I have to go along with his veto."

"Melody," I said, "that's nonsense. You've had two moderately successful CB radio songs, and since a major record company made some money on them, you should follow through with a third one. Don't worry about your image as a CB-radio singer. Your only concern should be getting the exposure the record company can give you by recording another song." In spite of what I said, Melody chose to follow her agent's advice. Until she understands the importance of image-building, she'll never become the celebrity she wants to be.

Conclusion

In this chapter, three completely different examples of image-building have been illustrated; two of them show how winning images are acquired, and the third shows how self-defeating a misunderstanding of the concept of image-building can be. Conscious effort to build a winning image makes a tremendous difference in achieving desirable results.

Perhaps the most important lesson to be learned here is that you must have a game plan. You will never achieve the image you desire simply by drifting. You *must* take a definite direction; building a winning image is really no different from any other busness venture. And to repeat, it's also important for you to realize *what* image you want before you exert any efforts to obtain it. By now you should comprehend what a winning image really is, and therefore you are ready to begin to build yours. Once you define the kind of winning image you will strive for, you should incorporate several strategies in your efforts to build it, and coordinate them to work simultaneously in the same direction.

As your business grows, don't be afraid to make changes. Certain techniques become outmoded as business conditions and lifestyles change, and you must be able to adjust to the times. Obviously, once you become a big success, you will have to use entirely different methods from those you used at first to project your winning image. Still, you must have a game plan or you will find yourself drifting without direction and your image will be left to fate, and surely nobody wants to reach the pinnacle of success only to allow fate to take over from there on. Unless you have complete control of your image, you will seriously risk losing what you have worked so hard to achieve. Therefore, you must always realize that *building a winning image is a lifetime project that never ceases*.

19   Changing an Image

I have been told that tearing down an existing building and starting from scratch is easier than remodeling an old structure. In image-building I, too, would rather start from scratch. Unfortunately, an existing image cannot be torn down as quickly as a building. Because an image is intangible, you cannot change it by removing it as you would a physical object. The previous chapter discussed ways of building an image. We'll now consider ways of changing an existing one. Changing an image means that you must change people's thinking about you, and this is difficult because their emotions, philosophies, and, in many cases, deep-rooted prejudices are involved.

Tru Blue, for example, has firmly established himself as one of the South's all-time great lovers. His swinger reputation has spread throughout both Florida and Georgia, and there isn't a single female clerk who doesn't expect Tru to go on the make for her when he enters her department. In fact, an older female buyer may feel somewhat insulted if Tru doesn't proposition her or, at the very least, give her a little pinch. As might be expected, however, poor Tru has had a few close calls with jealous husbands and boy friends, and he's succeeded in upsetting department heads and floor managers. Lately, in fact, he has been getting it from

all fronts. His wife Sue has received anonymous telephone calls about his romantic escapades, people have
complained to his sales manager about them, and several former girl-friend buyers have become somewhat
disenchanted with Lover Boy. Even Tru has become
disillusioned. He claims, "It's just not the same any-
more. I don't really have the good times I used to, and,
quite frankly, I'm too tired the next day. I guess I'm
getting a little too old to stay up all night and still be
able to knock 'em dead the next day!" While practically every other salesman in the territory thinks it
would be fabulous to be like Tru Blue for just two
weeks, Tru isn't at all happy with himself and wants
to change his image.

You've heard that a leopard never changes its
spots, and, unfortunately for Tru, so has everybody
with whom he deals in Georgia and Florida. Tru's first
thought was to request a change to a territory where
no one had any knowledge of the "Tru Blue legend."
His other alternative, he thought, would be to get into
another line of work so that he could stay in the same
area. When he checked out both options, Tru quickly
discovered that he would suffer a severe economic loss
by pursuing either, so a change just isn't practical. Besides, Tru dislikes the idea of running away from a
problem. As you can see, changing his image is not
going to be the easiest thing he's ever done.

My first suggestion to Tru is that he write down
exactly what image he wants. He should also record a
step-by-step game plan that he intends to follow in order to achieve this goal. A few of his initial changes
must be drastic so that everyone will immediately notice a definite difference. He needs this shock value in
order to get things rolling. His appearance is the sim-
plest thing to change, so getting a short haircut, putting
away his mod clothes, and buying a few conservative

business suits should be included in his initial priorities. Wearing his glasses when visiting his clientele will also help. With this appearance change, everyone will immediately notice a "new" Tru.

Simultaneously with the change in appearance, Tru has to change his vocabulary—no more sweet talk, no more addressing women as "baby doll" or "sweetheart." Taking his wife with him on trips occasionally will also benefit his image. Certainly, she should assist him at the regional ladies' apparel shows. Male customers should be Tru's only luncheon guests, and in order to show his gratitude for orders he gets, he should send a letter of appreciation afterward to each customer (something he has never done before). Both his radical change in appearance and his new business etiquette will eventually change Tru's image if he consistently adheres to his game plan. What is most important, however, is his application of the above recommendations on a day-to-day basis. He should *never* deviate from his game plan. He must remember that what he's doing is like working toward a sales quota or engaging in any other business venture. If he follows a definite pattern with conscious effort, even a losing image such as Tru Blue's can be changed.

Duane Twain, after six years in the big leagues, has earned the dubious reputation of being the "bad boy" of major league baseball. His bad image is well deserved, based as it is on his crazy antics, which include throwing pop bottles and beer cans back into the stands in the left field, throwing his bat at opposing pitchers, fighting with practically everyone, skipping practice, and not showing up at the ball park for as many as three days at a time. Either a psychoanalyst or his minister finally got through to Duane, because, believe it or not, he now wants to be known as a clean-cut, all-American athlete, who's a positive influence on youngsters. Duane loves his own children very much, and now that they're older, he doesn't want them to be ashamed of him. The horrible press coverage he's received over the past six years means that it's going to be a helluva job for Duane to convince the public that he's changed; but, if he wants it badly enough, he can eventually create a winning image.

Naturally, he'll have to start by behaving like a civilized human being. For anyone else, this may not seem so difficult, but Duane will definitely have to work hard at it. He must completely reverse his behavior by showing good sportsmanship and conducting himself like a gentleman while in the public eye. I suggested to him that he make an all-out effort to concentrate solely on playing good baseball, which would not only improve his game, but also help him to outgrow his poor image. As in other cases, only long-term performance will change Duane's image. Naturally, some fans will be disappointed when they see that he is *not* acting like a maniac, but in order to preserve both his major-league standing and his image, he must practice restraint and self-discipline. Otherwise, he's not going to be a big leaguer very much longer.

A winning image can also change an entire industry. Norman Traeger, a close personal friend of mine, decided to change the image of the roller skating industry so that he and his partner, Steve Haenel, could build an empire of roller skating rinks.

In 1970, Norman had taken his little daughters, Jamie and Jennifer, to a rink for an afternoon of fun. The roller rink was in an old Quonset hut-type building in a rundown neighborhood behind a used car lot. "The facilities were horrendous," says Norm. "In fact, the place was so filthy that you felt like putting toilet paper on the floor in front of the urinal in the men's room! The thing that really amazed me, though, was that there were four hundred people in this awful place who were actually enjoying themselves. I thought," he continued, "if these people could enjoy *this* place, just imagine the fun they would have if they were skating in a modern, clean facility." This idea gave Norman Traeger the motivation to start his company, United Skates of America, which, by 1975, became the largest roller skating business in the nation.

"In order to appreciate our story, Bob," he told me, "let me tell you about the history of the roller skating industry. Roller skating began in this country in the late 1800s, and by the early 1900s, it was a society sport as fashionable as tennis is today. However, the image of roller skating started to go downhill during World War I, and it continued to go from bad to worse through the fifties and sixties. You see, the rinks were family-owned and -operated businesses, and when the buildings began to deteriorate, these mom and pop owners weren't willing to modernize them, let alone keep them up. During the wars, servicemen found them good places to pick up girls. By the fifties, the image was even worse and the rinks were taken over by black-leather-jacket gangs. When it got this bad, family-oriented customers stayed away from the rinks, and these people are the market we're really after.

"In the meantime ice skating was growing by leaps and bounds. Roller skating had developed a roller derby image—you know, the 'Bay City Bomber'—but ice skating was enjoying an entirely different image because it had modern facilities and people like Peggy Fleming were in it. What had happened was that roller skating had become a sport for the lower classes while ice skating had become distinguished as a higher-class sport. When I compared both types of skating, I decided that roller skating had much more to offer for three reasons. First, it's easier to do; second, it's less tiring; and third, it's more fun!"

Once Norman had the idea, it wasn't quite so simple to convince a banker to give him the financing he needed. "My banker looked at me like I was crazy," he told me. "You see, roller skating was an invisible sport. Do you know, Bob, that there are more than thirty-five hundred rinks in the country—that's more than McDonald's hamburger restaurants, and I bet you can't think of more than one or two that you've seen in the past ten years. They are in terrible locations—behind used car lots in blighted areas and in other obscure places. Yet McDonald's restaurants, because of the locations, seem to be on practically every corner. It took a lot of hard selling to get the finances I needed to get my first rink under way, but we were finally able to do it."

Norman is the chairman of the board of United Skates of America, and he and Steve Haenel, the company's president, put together, in my opinion, one of the nation's all-time best image-building packages when they established their company. First, they created a good name (you should review Chapter 1, "What's in a Name?"), which, as Norm puts it, is a fun name. "United Skates of America is a name nobody will forget, and it immediately separates us from the rest of the industry because they've all got names like 'Rollarena,' 'Skateland,' or just plain old 'Norm and Steve's.'" The name also makes it easy to develop a theme, Norm points out. "For example, we use the colors red, white, and blue to decorate, and we have stars and stripes and patriotic emblems displayed at every rink. We even developed a character whom we call 'Uncle Skates,' who dresses up like Uncle Sam. The kids love him."

Secondly, Norm and Steve chose good locations. They bought or leased valuable properties near heavy-traffic, four-lane streets. Their imaginative, award-winning buildings were definitely superior to existing

Quonset-hut rinks. United Skates was also determined to dispel the fear that one's personal safety was in jeopardy when he went roller skating. A dress code as well as a conduct code was established. If a customer didn't follow the rules, he or she was firmly asked to leave. This certainly doesn't bother the customers because for everyone kid who had to be thrown out, United Skates picks up twenty long-term customers. Furthermore, each rink employs three off-duty policemen. One is stationed in the parking lot so that he is immediately visible to parents, who then feel confident that their children will be in no danger while on the premises. The other two work inside the building. The interior of the building is painstakingly maintained—the ultraclean rest rooms are inspected every half-hour, all floors—except, of course, the rink itself—are fully carpeted, and the carpeting is completely replaced every three years. The managers of United Skates are qualified, well-trained people who understand that they are *selling a good time*. "That's our reason for existence," Norman concludes.

Norman and Steve's outstanding achievement deserves a great deal of credit. Convincing bankers of the validity of their product, persuading prospective landowners to develop expensive buildings to be used by United Skates of America, and changing the poor image of roller skating rinks was a very difficult task. Yet they had a plan that was feasible, and while they proceeded to build their business, they also built their image (and changed the image of the sport as a whole). As pointed out in the chapter "Building an Image," achieving success depends on building an image at the same time you are building your business. Today, Norm and Steve are opening up new roller-skating rinks throughout the United States, and as they expand, they continue to improve the image of roller skating.

In 1934, Clark Gable also changed the image of an entire industry. In what was, for those days, a rather risqué bedroom scene with Claudette Colbert in the movie *It Happened One Night,* Gable removed his shirt, and, to the audience's surprise, he was not wearing an undershirt. His masculine image, it is reported, rocked the underwear industry beyond belief. As the movie broke box-office records, the purchasing of men's undershirts seemed to decrease proportionately.

Learning a good lesson from such an experience, manufacturers and retailers of hats feared that their industry's image would suffer when John F. Kennedy became President of the United States because he never wore a hat. Consequently, they requested him to "save the industry" by wearing one to his inauguration. After much coaxing, Kennedy finally agreed that he would at least carry a hat, even though he refused to wear it!

Without question, the public's image of anything can prove quite fickle. Policemen are considered "good guys" for a period of time; then their image changes and they become the "bad guys." Even the image of smoking marijuana has been subject to change. For many years, the public considered marijuana users low-life characters (hippies, yippies, and the like), but the image of marijuana slowly changed and it is now somewhat socially acceptable to smoke it. While the PTA and the Surgeon General still aren't endorsing it, the public's attitude toward marijuana has altered so significantly that possession in many states is no longer a felony.

It's interesting to see how many groups have been attacking the giant corporations in America. For a while, the big-company image was considered a nega-

A Fable For Now:

Of Mice and Mammoths

The elephant is a remarkable animal. He is
a huge beast, yet can move quickly in an emer-
gency. He is stronger than man, yet will work
hard for man. His great weight can crush any
human being, but his trunk can take a peanut
from a child's hand.

He is, all in all, a unique creature.

One day, when one of these most unusual
beasts was strolling through the jungle, munch-
ing leaves as he walked, he was accosted by a
mouse.

Now this mouse was not your ordinary ro-
dent, but a spokesmouse for all the little animals
in the jungle. As such, he occasionally felt the
need to correct whatever he thought was wrong
with the system. To the mouse, the elephant was
a problem. A big problem.

"Your pardon, Pachyderm," the mouse said
to the startled elephant, "but I'm going to dis-
member you. You have simply grown too big for
the rest of us in the jungle and take up more than
your share of space."

"*Àu contraire,*" the elephant responded, "I
don't know where you get your figures, but there
are nearly 8,000 other animals eating from the
same trees as I and drinking from the same water

©1976 Mobil Oil Corporation

holes. I have not stopped them from doing that despite my great size. And I know for a fact that the smaller animals occupy a larger share of the jungle now than they did 10 years ago.

"So, I think, friend Mouse, you ought to look again at what you propose. First, from the standpoint of fact, and then to decide what purpose would be served by dismembering me."

Before the mouse could answer, there was a thundering, shattering roar and a large tree toppled and crashed to the earth. Before the mouse could move, it had landed directly on his long, straight—or, at least formerly straight—tail.

"Elephant," the mouse roared, "don't just stand there; do something!"

"Why don't you ask one of the smaller animals?" the elephant retorted. "Why ask a big, bulky, brawny behemoth like me?"

"Because there are some things only the largest of animals can handle. There is no other animal capable of removing this burdensome bush from my once-straight tail," the mouse answered meekly.

"Just checking, Mouse; just checking," the elephant said. "I would have helped you in either case, but I thought it would be better if you saw the error of your ways yourself. And by the way," he added, "think what a fine fix you would be in if I had been dismembered *before* the tree fell."

Moral: Nobody should assume that BIG spells BAD. Though some in Congress would break up some oil companies as too big, the job of fueling America requires bigness. Besides, petroleum is one of the least concentrated industries: less so, for example, than autos, steel or network television. At last count, there were some 8,000 petroleum producers and 133 refiners. And that's no fable.

Mobil

tive one. Being big was bad. Had the giant corporations of America not fought this attack on their
existence, eventually we would have seen their downfall, which would have been a calamity for America
because many of our most important but smaller-sized
industries depend upon the ability of the giants to
operate them. For example, a company must be gar-
gantuan in order to manufacture automobiles, airplanes, television sets, and steamships, or to refine oil.
Because of the public's demand for products such as
these, being big is a positive factor, and recently, a
great number of major companies have been spending
large sums of money to inform the public of how vital
the big corporations are to the well-being of our free
enterprise system. One such message by Mobil Oil
Corporation appeared not long ago in *The Wall Street
Journal* (see previous page). Although it was costly
and not directly connected with the marketing of its
product, Mobil was willing to run it as a public service. Such messages by concerned corporations can
benefit everyone by effectively altering certain images
that have been wrongfully distorted.

I have emphasized the importance of changing a losing image to a winning one. Yet there are times
when you may simply wish to change an image because it no longer serves your purposes. A good example of this is Downs' Furniture Store, which is
owned and operated by Mark Downs. For years, the
business has sold popular-priced merchandise in a
middle-income area, but as the neighborhood slowly
deteriorated, business decreased. Now Mark Downs
would like to upgrade his trade and move to a different
location. Though changing an existing image to a new
image is difficult, Downs can follow a definite course
of action in order to give his business a complete
facelift. A change to a new location is an excellent

start, and in this connection I would recommend that
Mark read Chapter 5, "Going First Class," before he
signs a new lease. The right shopping center will make
a tremendous difference in attracting the type of customer he wants to cater to, and the decor of his new
store will have to be considerably different from that
of the old one. Mark will also have to gear his advertising to a different market. And naturally, he will
have to establish new contacts with different manufacturers of fine furniture to obtain new lines. Making
major changes, some almost equivalent to those required when starting a different business, will enable
Mark to change his image to the one he desires.

Robin Wood also wants to change his image. He
has just been promoted to the position of vice president
in a major tire company, and it's possible that he may
one day become president of the firm. Robin worked
so hard for his promotion that he never had time to
develop any close friendships within the corporation,
and the present chairman of the board thinks Robin
must develop a closer rapport with his associates if he
is to be considered seriously as a candidate for the
presidency. "Robin, you must change that stuffed-
shirt, pompous image you project to the rest of the
team," the chairman has told him. "You have to be
more relaxed if you want to come across more effectively with the other men in management, or you'll
never be able to motivate them effectively as the president."

Robin has a beautiful and charming wife, Holly, and
I suggested that she could be a great asset to him in
getting to know his people better. Holly can throw delightful dinner parties, and if Robin puts to use some
of the tips offered in Chapter 14, "The Having-a-
Sense-of-Humor Image," together with those in
Chapter 12, "Your Spouse—an Asset or a Liability,"

"You gotta give them credit for trying to change their image."

I am betting he'll be capable of rehauling his image and getting the job he's after.

As you can see, changing an image is a difficult but attainable objective. It's considerably more difficult than building an image from scratch because you must change the thinking of others, and this will be a time-consuming task. You must also be absolutely certain that the image you're aiming for is really the most desirable one for you. I have known many people who want to change their images because "the grass seemed greener. . . ." Yet once they made the change, they weren't at all happy and wanted their old image back again! Such a change of heart can often be financially and personally damaging. Crystal Clare, one of television's all-time best comedienne/singer personalities, at the height of her career, switched to motion pictures and tried to change her image to that of a sex symbol. As a sex goddess, she was a miserable flop, and she would have given anything to recapture the good, clean image she had formerly enjoyed. What happened here was that Crystal, unfortunately, did not give sufficient thought to the change she had in mind. Had she done so, she would have realized that she just wasn't sex-goddess material. Nor would she have ignored the warnings by her agent and close friends that she was being foolhardy. So she allowed her ego to dictate what turned out to be a disastrous change in image.

Conclusion

The importance of having a definite game plan before you make a change cannot be overstressed because *changing your image* can mean changing your life forever. When the stakes are that high, you'd better be certain you do a good job!

20 Extra Winning-
Image Tips

Before concluding *Winning Images*, I want to add a few *extra* tips that will help you to acquire a better image. I hope you do not think they are less important for being "thrown into" a miscellaneous chapter. Actually, although each tip is worthwhile, it is not a broad enough subject by itself to expand into a complete chapter.

First, always be on time for appointments. Punctuality, an admirable trait, is rare; yet it is really nothing more than showing the other person that you respect him or her. When somebody shows up late for an appointment, the party who had to wait may very well look upon the lateness as an insult, for it signals the message: "So what if I got here late? I just didn't care enough to be concerned about causing you any inconvenience to make sure that I got here on time!" Barring a serious accident or sudden sickness, there is *never* an adequate excuse for being late. If the completely unexpected does occur (an air flight is canceled, your car is stolen, a bridge collapses, or the like), there is always a phone available to let the other person know you're going to be delayed. Punctuality is a winning-image builder that required only conscientious effort before it becomes a way of life.

Another excellent trait to acquire is the knack of remembering names. It has often been said that the sweetest sound any man hears is his own name, and if you put forth a sincere effort, you'll surprise even yourself with your ability to remember people's names. There are techniques you can develop, and *everyone* should make a firm resolution to master this art. Pick up a book on the subject at a bookstore or library. Most of the systems for this specific kind of memorization suggest associating names with pictures or ridiculous sounds and phrases that will instantly call the correct name to mind. Once you develop this skill, for the rest of your life others will be impressed that you cared enough to remember their names.

I'll never forget how shocked I was when I visited Worldly Cosmetics Corporation and was given a tour of the plant by the president, Elmer Fudge. As we drove through the huge facilities of the company on a golf cart, I was amazed by Fudge's inability to call a single employee by his name. I sensed an air of resentment toward him on the part of his employees, and since many of the older ones had been with his company for over twenty years, I could easily understand why they would be upset with Fudge for not even acknowledging them by name!

When I was first out of college, I attended the wedding of a close friend who was marrying a very wealthy woman. Her grandfather, Ben Factor, was the chairman of the board of Wear's, one of the nation's largest department stores. "Big Ben," as he was affectionately called, stood in the reception line as literally hundreds of guests, whom he was meeting for the first time, passed by. As they aproached, he would greet each with a few words and then turn to the next person. During the dinner, Big Ben tablehopped and chatted, and not only remembered each guest by name, but was able to recall their earlier brief conversation. "How's the golf game, Larry?" he would comment to one guest. "Say, Jackie, that's a beautiful gown you're wearing. How do you like our city? Have you been able to see our wonderful art gallery yet?" "How's the real estate business coming along these days, Jerry?" "Eddie, I think you're going to do real well in the insurance business. It's a wonderful field." I might add that the guests at the wedding were more impressed with Grandpa "Big Ben" than they were with the bride. To this day, when there's a conversation about the wedding, or when someone brings up the subject of Wear's Department Stores, anybody who was at the wedding will comment about what a great guy Big Ben is. The fact that he was thoughtful enough to take the effort to develop a memory technique for remembering names is what impressed me so much about him.

At another wedding I attended, Timothy Burr, the president of a large lumber company and the proud father of the bride, decided to give a speech. He spoke for thirty boring minutes. Tim Burr, who was kiddingly referred to as "Tiny Tim" (he was quite large), was a very poor speaker, and not only was his speech a failure, but it almost ruined the whole occasion and made him look like a fool. I have always believed that it's better for people to wonder why you didn't speak than to wonder why you did. Somebody should have mentioned this to Tiny Tim before his daughter's wedding reception.

I have seen many important leaders of business and industry lower their esteem in the eyes of their audience by making inadequately prepared or sloppily delivered speeches. Rarely is a nonprofessional speaker capable of delivering a good speech without a great deal of effort and preparation. Because people see professional speakers on television every day, anyone asked to give an occasional speech is up against a great deal of competition, and unless he's fully prepared, he's going to fall flat on his face. Depending on the subject, most speakers like to keep their audiences awake by throwing in bits of humor. However, many speakers try too hard, and as a result, they "lay an egg." Always remember that you're not a comedian, and only a handful of people have the talent to make a good living by getting up in front of an audience and acting funny. Humor can be injected into practically any speech but it is important that you practice your timing and *be certain that you are using good material*. Also, don't be afraid to "steal" somebody else's funny lines. You can find a few good quotes to tie into your speech by reading toastmaster or joke books. While you are preparing your speech (weeks in advance, I advise), record any joke, story, or event you hear or experience that might be applicable to your speech. You'll be surprised at the amount of good material you'll come up with if you stay on the alert.

Getting back to my philosophy that "it's better to have people wonder why you didn't speak rather than to wonder why you did," let me tell you a story about a talk show I appeared on in Memphis to discuss my book, *Total Commitment*. A few minutes before the show was about to start, the hostess said, "Bob, I have a great idea. Why don't you sit in for the whole hour of our show, and you can interject comments while I talk with my other guests."

"What's the subject your guests will be discussing?" I asked.

She replied, "Oh, it's going to be a fascinating conversation. One gentleman is from Russia and the other is from Australia, and we're going to compare the different lifestyles and governments of the two nations. Come on, Bob, you'll have a good time."

Amazed at her suggestion, I said, "Look, you invited me to be a guest on your show to discuss my book, and I'm thoroughly prepared to do that. I am an expert on this subject, and there are two things I can do better than any other human being in the world. First, I can read my own handwriting better than anyone else, and second, I know more about my book than any other person on the face of the earth. On the other hand, I know absolutely nothing about Russia and Australia—at least no more than anyone else who will be in your audience. And yet you want me to go on television and talk with experts about two countries I have never even been to. You must be kidding!"

Since she realized I was right, I appeared as a solo act during the second part of the show and had a very fine interview concerning the one subject I was prepared to discuss on television that particular morning. I honestly believe that by doing it this way, all involved got their money's worth, and I suppose the fact that I was invited back for an interview concerning my next book indicates that the talk show's producer was satisfied, too.

Another tip I want to offer is that your image can be greatly affected by the people with whom you associate. While I'm not saying that you should drop your friends because they're not good for your image, there is much to be said about the image you will project based on the company you keep. The expressions "Birds of a feather flock together" and "If you sleep with dogs you'll get up with fleas" are not merely idle phrases. Both adages are quite true, particularly from the point of view of how others will react. For example, if you have very important and successful friends, people will think, "He must have something on the ball to run around with those people." And if your friends are all losers, though this may not seriously hurt your image, it won't be a positive influence either. Of course, if you're constantly seen in the company of disreputable people, your image will suffer badly. The last thing in the world I want to suggest is that you change friends in order to build a better image (social climbing is a contemptible habit of too many people), but be aware of the image impact to be gained or lost from the people with whom you associate.

I also want to brief you on the "winner's image." A good example is the image the New York Yankees had during the fifties when they dominated baseball. Because many individual athletes have this quality, they intimidate their opponents to such an extent that they have a strong extra edge before even entering a sports contest. Athletes, in these instances, refer to their opponents as being "psyched out." UCLA's great basketball teams under Coach John Wooden had this winner's-image edge going for them, and so has Ohio State, particularly when they're playing at Ohio Stadium! The winner's image can be applied to many areas. For example, a Xerox salesman may have this edge when he competes with an off-brand copying machine salesman. And the IBM salesman will have it going for him when he is in a selling situation with a small, unknown computer company. A "Big Eight" accounting firm has it when dealing with a small ac-

"Birds of a feather flock together."

counting firm that has a mutual client. And the attorney who represents the giant law firm has this edge when he deals with an attorney who represents his client's opposition in discussing a possible lawsuit. It is important that you be aware of the winner's image, because if you do have it, you should flaunt it. And if you don't have it, it is imperative that you recognize it and know how to work around people who may otherwise intimidate you with their winner's image.

An experience I recently had in Pittsburgh holds a good lesson for everyone—especially for cities. I was taking a taxi from the airport to the Hilton Hotel in the downtown area, but because of road repairs, a twenty-five-minute trip took more than an hour. While tied up in a traffic jam, my fit-to-be-tied cab driver interrupted his cussing and swearing long enough to say to me, "Mister, I don't know where you're from, but the one good thing about Pittsburgh is that it makes people appreciate their own hometown!"

The cabbie then launched into what seemed like a well-rehearsed speech about Pittsburgh, which he'd undoubtedly made hundreds of times before. "You see those potholes in the road they're workin' on, mister? Well, they oughta rename this city and call it 'Potsburgh.' Why, the damn politicians are so crooked here that they must get a kickback everytime they repave this road. Ya know, they done the job just a couple a years ago! No wonder our taxes are so high in this town." He proceeded to tell me that Pittsburgh's taxes are among the worst in the country, and from there he went on to complain about every single bad thing you could possibly think about a city. Although I believe in free speech, I finally had to tell him to "shut up." I firmly believe that no person should knock any place from which he derives his livelihood, but if you look around, you'll discover how many people violate this rule every day of their lives. If I owned a limousine service or a taxi company, I would hire people to periodically spot-check my drivers to find out what they were saying about the city to passengers, and anyone who was not being, in effect, a goodwill ambassador, would soon be looking for another job.

Nothing is worse for a business's image than to have one of the employees bad-mouthing the company, and every business should set up controls to prevent this. There's enough competition in this world, and the last thing you need is to be pulled down from the inside! Unless employees' gripes are revealed to management, they will definitely do severe harm to the company's image.

A good tip for the bus industry may also be applicable to your own business. I can't understand why bus companies don't try to upgrade their images by moving their terminals to more desirable places. Taking a bus for a distance of one hundred to three hundred miles may be a very enjoyable and economical way for many people to travel, but I suspect that the one thing that discourages more people from traveling by bus is the poor location of most bus terminals. A person will undoubtedly be afraid to walk through a decrepit neighborhood to the terminal and, once there, will not relish waiting around for the bus for what might be a long time. The majority of bus terminals are located in inner-city areas just off the main streets of the downtown section. They make excellent refuges for alcoholics, drug addicts, and other dregs of society. How much better it would be to move the terminals to a suburban section just outside the downtown area.

I also recommend that publicly owned companies employ a good public relations firm to produce their annual reports *during the good years*. When earnings are down, companies should use the same firms but purposely avoid any extravagance that will create the impression that the company is spending money on frivolous matters—that is, they should go easy on expenses during bad years. Many stockholders are small investors, and they'll get upset if they think that money is being poorly spent when the company has a drop in earnings or losses for the year.

Keeping in good physical condition is another good tip to pass on to you for your winning image. A trim person certainly makes a better first impression than an overweight or slovenly one. Being in good shape at all times has even more important advantages. When you're in good health, you'll have the extra stamina that will provide you with additional motivation and drive. Psychologically, you'll have an edge on the next guy because when you feel good you generate excitement and enthusiasm. The man who's below par will have little energy, and he'll have a perpetual rundown look that will be noticed by everyone.

When I am in the process of writing a manuscript, I need the mental alertness to work long, tedious hours. You've heard of an athlete getting down to his fighting weight—I get down to my "writing weight." I always exercise every day, but when I am writing a book, I increase my physical conditioning program so that I have the extra stamina to work longer hours and operate on less sleep. Normally I average seven hours of sleep per night, but when writing a manuscript, I cut that down to an average of four. If I were not in such good physical condition, I would never be able to maintain this pace without having it affect both my business career and my writing.

Another image I want to briefly mention is the "father image" that exists in many employer-employee relationships. It's important for you to be aware of this image, particularly if you are the employer or manager of other people. In order to be effective with some types of employees, you must realize that you automatically project a father image, and he or she will expect you to conduct yourself in a paternal way. I bring this matter to your attention because if you fail to recognize the employees who need this image, you will not be able to deal with them effectively. I first learned about this when I was twenty-five years old. At that time I employed a salesman who was fifty-one years old and a retired chief warrant officer of the army. Floyd Lloyd would affectionately call me the "old man," a holdover expression from the military where it is commonly used when referring to the commanding officer. I would have sloughed this expression off as army jargon except for the fact that Floyd always came to me for fatherly advice. He would ask my opinion on everything, from how to raise his children (who were nearly my age at that time), to what to do when he and his wife weren't getting along. I learned a valuable lesson while working with Floyd, because as the years have gone by, hundreds of men have come to me for similar advice. Wives whose husbands had drinking problems have called me, men have come to me for guidance about whether or not to get divorced, other married men have sought my advice on how to work out problems with their girl friends, and husbands and wives have asked me to help them with their family budgets! It's important for you to realize the value of this kind of responsibility because certain people in this world *need* an employer for a father image. If you don't provide them with one, they will be frustrated and may discontinue working for you because this subconscious need is not being fulfilled.

You should be aware of one other type of image

"We came to this country to escape religious persecution. Of course, this is your land. Indians will never know on a firsthand basis what it's like to be a minority group."

even though you may never want to use it. I call it the "controversial image." I have known many individuals who thrive on being controversial, and they succeed in building a winning image through controversy. April Phouls, a highly successful novelist, has built her image around being controversial, and she is much in demand as a guest on radio and TV shows because of her sometimes outlandish yet intelligent opinions. April will dispute any popular opinion; she'll attack anything and anybody. Her thoughts are highly provocative, and although I disagree with practically everything she says, I find her an exciting personality and other people obviously have the same opinion of her.

Like the "controversial type," the "celebrity type" also projects a unique image. Have you ever wondered why one celebrity enjoys many years of tremendous popularity while another is tagged as being over the hill and fades into oblivion? Again, we can understand this phenomenon in terms of a winning image. Those who have one will certainly fulfill many more ambitions than those who don't. The latter will eventually die a slow death by living the remaining years of their lives in the past. Such a circumstance can make a tremendous difference to an individual's state of mind and welfare for as many as twenty to thirty years after he or she has hit the peak. It is not merely chance or "the draw of the card" that determines such fate. You can be the master of your own fate and influence the way people regard you. Thankfully, each of us *can* be the decisive factor; we don't have to depend on luck.

Once you have a winning image, it can carry you through periods when your performance might not be worthy of the usual image you project. For example, a famous artist can do an occasional poor painting, but if his image is good enough, the public will still buy his work. Or a professional singer can have an off night, but his reputation will pull him through. Even a judge can hand down the wrong decision, but it will be accepted because of his past record.

Perhaps after reading the extra tips in this chapter you will conclude that there is much more to be said about images. If so, you have developed an "awareness" and are now on your way to a *winning image*.

21   A Winning Image

"In Heaven an angel is nobody in particular."
—George Bernard Shaw

Perhaps when we get to heaven we can at last stop concerning ourselves with a winning image, but in the meantime, I, and perhaps by now you, too, believe that everyone who wants to achieve anything of significance will accomplish it more effectively with a winning image. And, as relative as the word "winning" may be, I hope this book has made it clear what images are all about, how to differentiate between a winning and a losing image, and how to get the winning image you want.

As explained in the chapter "Building a Winning Image," you must commit the image you want to a written, clear, and concise plan, and, at the same time, you must correlate it with the development of your career. Always remember that you're building two things at the same time—your career and your image. And never, ever, separate them!

As you begin your own winning-image-building program, let me stress again that a winning image must be based on both integrity and sincerity. By far the worst image is the so-called winning image that is built on and sustained by fraud. Though one cannot be faulted too much for making minor exaggerations in order to create initial interest, be warned that there is a thin line between this kind of "selling" and actual misrepresentation. You know the difference between right and wrong, so this matter must be left to your discretion.

Also, if you have a losing image, don't expect to attain a winning one without first making drastic and major changes. You must completely erase your losing image, and a great deal of time and *actual performance* will be required before you'll be able to establish the credibility needed to achieve a new image.

Take, for example, the Wicked Witch of the West in L. Frank Baum's *The Wonderful Wizard of Oz.** I believe even she can develop a winning image, though she'll have to work very hard to convince the Munchkins that she is, indeed, a good witch. She can do this, though, if she performs a lot of good deeds. She must be very consistent in her performance, for even the slightest deviation can frighten the dubious Munchkins into believing in the old losing image they had of her. My first suggesstion to her would be to perform some "magic" and make sure that Dorothy and Toto are returned safely to Kansas. Next, she should give the Scarecrow a brain, the Tin Woodman

---

* L. Frank Baum, *The Wonderful Wizard of Oz* (George M. Hill Company, 1900).

a heart, and the Cowardly Lion all the courage he wants. Of course, she'll have to sell herself to the Munchkins and the people of Emerald City, so she'll have to grant them a few wishes, too. If there is anyone who needs to apply my Credibility Principle, she is the one!

While the Wicked Witch is being a good girl, I think she'll also have to clean up her act by changing her name. Somehow, I just don't feel comfortable with the "Wicked Witch" theme. And since I am not overly fond of her black dresses, she's going to have to go on a shopping spree on Fifth Avenue. I'll also hint that she should disregard her broom and fly by commercial airlines—first class, naturally! I don't know how to tell her this, but while she's in New York, she's going to have to visit a beauty spa. She may have to spend a few days there, but I am sure the results will be well worth the time it takes to produce them.

While her castle lends itself to stability, the Wicked Witch may want to do some remodeling. Quite frankly her present castle gives me the willies! A few Henny Youngman jokes will brighten up the rather coarse way in which she presently expresses herself, and she's going to have to stop intimidating people. Although I do not normally like the idea of women wearing low-cut dresses or see-through blouses during working hours, I do think this old gal definitely needs a little sex appeal.

Another thing she's going to have to stop is that disappearing act she performs when she takes off on her broom in a cloud of smoke. After all, she's only making it more difficult to determine whether she's a real image or a mirage!

If there's hope for the Wicked Witch of the West, then there's always room for each of us to improve our image if we really want to. Once you begin your journey toward a winning image, you must travel on this same path for the rest of your life. To show that I practice what I preach, I ask each and every one of you who enjoyed this book to join in extending your individual gratitude by passing along the good word about *Winning Images* to all your friends and associates. By doing this, you will aid me in *my* constant goal to build *my* winning image.

I thank each of you who does build a winning image, because in the process you are making this a better world for all of us.

Non-Fiction Bestsellers from POCKET BOOKS

___ 82343 BLIND AMBITION John Dean $2.75

___ 81499 ENOLA GAY Gordon Thomas and Max Morgan Witts $2.50

___ 81289 EVERYTHING YOU ALWAYS WANTED TO KNOW ABOUT ENERGY (BUT WERE TOO WEAK TO ASK) Naura Hayden $1.95

___ 81424 GO OUT IN JOY! Nina Herrmann $1.95

___ 81423 HOW TO CURE YOURSELF OF POSITIVE THINKING Donald G. Smith $1.50

___ 82374 IMPROVING YOUR CHILD'S BEHAVIOR CHEMISTRY Lendon Smith, M.D. $2.25

___ 81733 LONG LIVE THE KING: A BIOGRAPHY OF CLARK GABLE Lyn Tornabene $2.50

___ 82368 THE RIGHT AND THE POWER Leon Jaworski $2.75

___ 81910 SYSTEMANTICS John Gall $1.95

___ 82054 TALKING TO MYSELF Studs Terkel $2.50

___ 81957 VIVIEN LEIGH Anne Edwards $2.50

Distinguished Non-Fiction from Pocket Books

a DNF 5-78